Map adapted from *With C...*
published b...

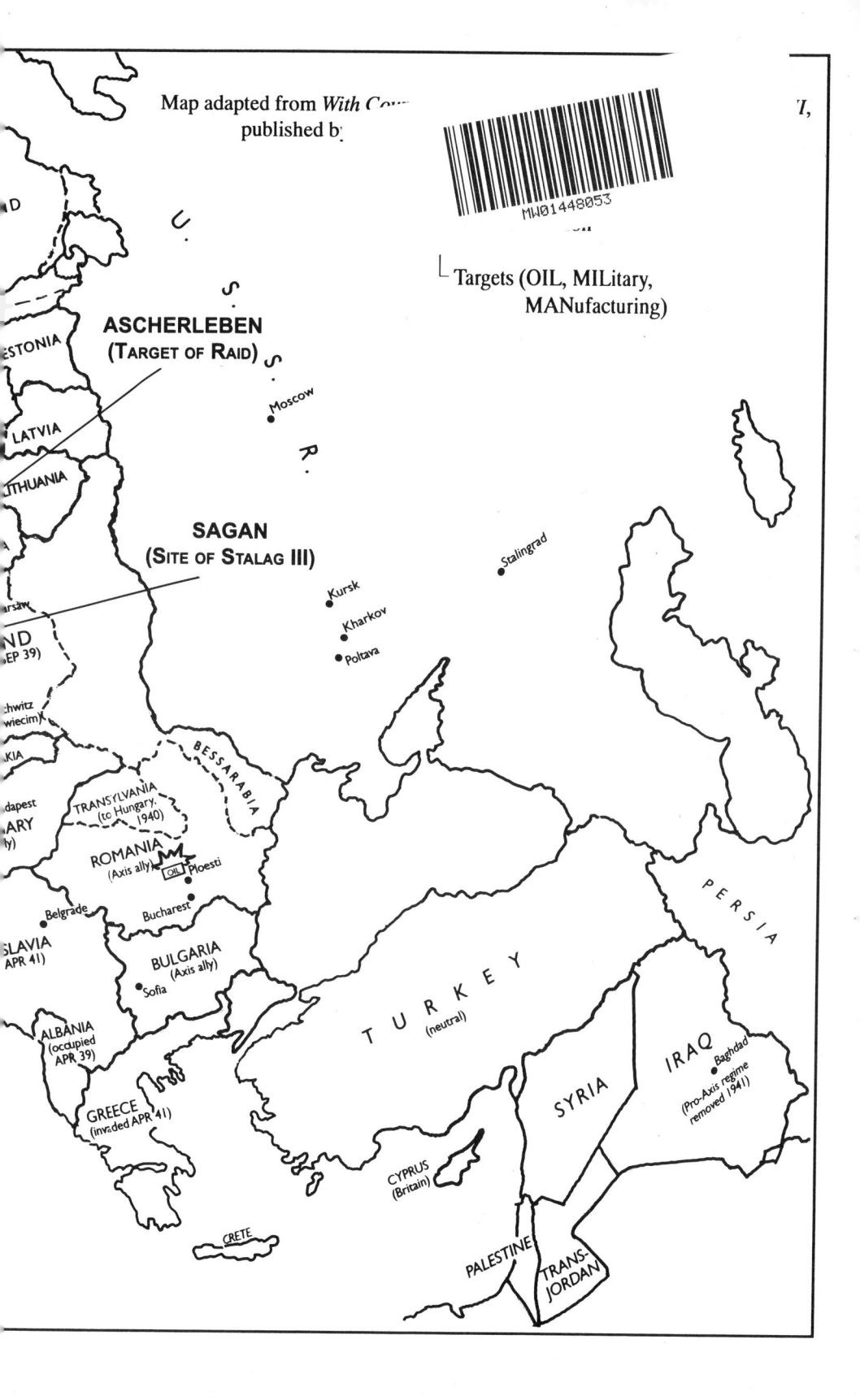

Targets (OIL, MILitary, MANufacturing)

ASCHERLEBEN
(Target of Raid)

SAGAN
(Site of Stalag III)

U.S.S.R.
• Moscow
• Stalingrad
• Kursk
• Kharkov
• Poltava

ESTONIA
LATVIA
LITHUANIA

...ND
(...EP 39)
...chwitz
...wiecim)
...KIA
...dapest
...ARY
...ly)

BESSARABIA
TRANSYLVANIA
(to Hungary, 1940)
ROMANIA
(Axis ally) OIL • Ploesti
• Belgrade
• Bucharest
...SLAVIA
(APR 41)
BULGARIA
(Axis ally)
• Sofia
ALBANIA
(occupied APR 39)
GREECE
(invaded APR 41)
CRETE

TURKEY
(neutral)

PERSIA

CYPRUS
(Britain)

SYRIA

IRAQ
• Baghdad
(Pro-Axis regime removed 1941)

PALESTINE
TRANS-JORDAN

The Wrong Side of the Fence

♦

A United States Army Air Corps POW in World War II

Our crew—all captured after mission—taken just before takeoff for European Theater of Operations, May, 1944, in front of B-24:

Standing, left to right—Sergeants Hart, Currie, Santora (radio operator); Moos; Leonard and Sorenson (engineer). Front row, left to right—Second Lieutenants Cole, (pilot); Post, (co-pilot); Smart (bombardier); Halmos, (navigator).

The Wrong Side of the Fence

◆

A United States Army Air Corps POW in World War II

Eugene E. Halmos, Jr.

White Mane Publishing Company, Inc.

Copyright © 1996 Eugene E. Halmos, Jr.

ALL RIGHTS RESERVED—No part of this book may be reproduced in any form without permission in writing from the publisher, except by a reviewer who wishes to quote brief passages in connection with a review.

Unless otherwise noted, all photos are courtesy of United States Air Force Academy, Colorado Springs, Colorado, from captured German documents and files.

This White Mane Publishing Company, Inc. publication was printed by:
Beidel Printing House, Inc.
63 West Burd Street
Shippensburg, PA 17257 USA

In respect for the scholarship contained herein, the acid-free paper used in this book meets the guidelines for permanence and durability of the Committee on Production Guidelines for Book Longevity of the Council on Library Resources.

For a complete list of available publications please write:
White Mane Publishing Company, Inc.
P.O. Box 152
Shippensburg, PA 17257-0152

Library of Congress Cataloging-in-Publication Data

Halmos, E. E.
   The wrong side of the fence : a United States Army Corps POW in World War II / Eugene E. Halmos, Jr.
     p.   cm.
   Includes index.
   ISBN 1-57249-034-9 (alk. paper)
   1. Halmos, E. E. 2. Stalag Luft 3 (Zagań, Poland : Concentration camp) 3. World War, 1939-1945--Personal narratives, American. 4. Prisoners of war--Poland--Biography. I. Title.
D805.P7H35 1996
940.54'7243'094381--dc20   96-10220
                                                                      CIP

PRINTED IN THE UNITED STATES OF AMERICA

For Ann

Who waited so faithfully and patiently for all this to be over

*It was always with us—that fence—
and we were on the wrong side of it.*

*Those 14-foot high, double rows of ugly,
rusting barbed wire, thoroughly electrified
and dominated by the gaunt,
four-legged guard towers with their machine guns,
searchlights, and ever-present German guards—
put a period to our every thought and dream,
circumscribed our world into a narrow space.*

*It made for monotony, the fence did—
monotony and tremendous pressure,
because a man couldn't escape it,
nor could he escape his companions
and his own thoughts.*

Table of Contents

Foreword .... **xiii**
Introduction .... **xiv**

1 June, 1944 .... **1**

    Some background; assembly for final mission, Flight to target and bombing, hit by flak—Parachute jump—Capture—First days of captivity.

2 July, 1944 .... **11**

    Interrogation—Camp and interrogation at Oberursel, Wetzlar—Solitary confinement—Leaving for Sagan—Description of Stalag III—Beginning of "Tin Can Carpentry."

3 August, 1944 .... **25**

    Life in Prison Camp, keeping "busy" —"Food" supplies —A system of exchange—Hopes for future and release—New "purge" arrives—No sign of Dave Smart—Problems with flies and other flying bugs—My Birthday—How German propaganda machine works—Statistics on number of prisoners.

4 September, 1944 .... **45**

    Living with flying bugs—Haircuts and Whiskers—Labor Day—Half-Rations to be enforced—How many prisoners got out of their damaged planes—Cold, damp weather—Timoshenka, the Cat, and kittens—Military formations for "Appels" and other requirements—Food getting short, hot meals hard to find—More on German propaganda—Air Raids begin to occur—More on "Tin Can Carpentry," construction of stoves and cooking devices—News sounds good, Allied paratroop landings in Holland—Less outdoor activity as weather gets colder—Army friendships, fickle and fleeting.

5 October, 1944 .... **56**

    How we handle the inclement weather—Cold, no heat, little warm covering—Dressing up to go to bed—Diphtheria in camp—Germans plan to increase prisoner population by 4,000 men—Bridge tournament—Letters from Home tell of "excellent treatment" by Germans, according to what home-folks have been told—Big Offensive seems to have started in West—Church services Sundays—

Table of Contents

Letter passed along to me—Mother to Colonel Spivey—Omens and portents became important—Santora reported OK—Total of 6,360 Americans in this camp—Weather continues bad, but Russians advance—Parcels come in from home—Need for bath, food, work—News slows down.

6 November, 1944   66

More prisoners come in—Now 160 in barracks—On half-rations—Longing for end of war and home—Learning to make quilts—Election Day in U.S. has little effect, but Roosevelt clear favorite here—Kittens, now cats, become problem—Germans acknowledge Roosevelt re-election—Armistice Day—Food situation easing—More prisoners come in, still no Dave Smart—Post learns he is a father—More parcels from home—Snow comes, mud becomes problem—Why news is all-important to us—Rain, bad weather persists—Hope for the final battle—Final thrust by Allies—Preparing for Thanksgiving, and whatever celebration we can mount.

7 December, 1944   75

We've been prisoners more than 5 months—Reminiscences of Thanksgiving—Remembering Pearl Harbor—Allies continue to advance, but slowly—Reading books, history, biography, the Bible—Food situation not good—We make ice cream—Germans promise beer for Xmas, at outrageous prices—Start to raise, then quickly dispose of mustache—German publications now showing possibility of defeat—Sleeping (trying to) completely dressed for warmth—First mail from home—News of "Battle of Bulge"—First three prisoners hospitalized for "nervous breakdown," remarkable record—Letters from home, Post and Cole get none—Cold weather, ice skating—Sleeping very difficult—Xmas celebrations, even for Germans—Families visit guard troops—Russians moving steadily toward us—A perfect Bridge hand.

8 January, 1945   84

Snowing heavily—Laundry chores—Post gets mail from home—I become cook—Hitler-Goebbels speeches, trying to raise spirits, hope—Successful escape—Dentist fixes teeth—Fighting over division of food—Shaved heads reappear—Searchlights in compound at night, plus dogs—What we might do if Russians reach us first—My watch fixed—Inter-compound visits to other camps in complex—British Xmas parcels distributed—Shoes become available—Germans begin evacuating camps and airfields around us, rumors that we must also move—Trying to save food for possible march—Letters from home mention Frank Hart, one of our gunners, whom

Table of Contents

we have not heard of—"Colonel Spivey" haircuts—Evacuation of camp starts, move out, afoot in snow and ice—Very miserable.

9   February, 1945   **97**

Walking through snow, dragging belongings, many refugees; afraid to stop for fear of freezing to death, no food, little water, nothing else—Staying in old brick kiln—Warm for once, but no water or anything else—Small towns almost deserted except for kids, old folks, and women—Prisoners almost take over small town—Arrival (via awful train ride) at Munich and Moosburg where camp is final stop—Trading for water and food—Hungarian troops encountered—General, colonels, top brass removed from us by Germans—Moosburg a dump—Delousing futile—Near-riot for water—Easy pickings among railroad officials—Camp even worse than Sagan, barracks worse and dirtier, more crowded, no heat, no water—Cursory search, more fumigation, showers and evidence of how much weight we've lost—No hot food—Some organization of our own, finally—Some sunshine, finally; some attempts to clean ourselves; starting tin can carpentry again, since no utensils of any kind—St. Valentine's Day—My own wedding anniversary—Lt. Paul George joins our "combine" as cook helping me—Lice and other biting vermin become intimate companions—News of Roosevelt-Churchill-Stalin Meeting—Building our own gas-powered stoves—Prisoners "strike" to force Germans to empty toilet areas—News getting better, Allies closer to us—Food supplies, even Red Cross packages, getting low—More on new type stoves we've built—Germans showing more and more confusions, disorganization—Continued cold—Food supplies tougher and tougher—Red Cross reaches us with some food packages—First "end of war" excitement.

10   March, 1945   **114**

Air raids get closer—Getting a lot of cooking utensils built—No baths despite German promises—German army a sloppy bunch—Patton's Third army now at Frankfurt, near us—German guard shoots, kills, South African private—Bartering among prisoners and troops—Rumors abound—More men come in from other camps—Some classmates of mine from training school in States—Air raids close, prisoners overrunning camp, but Germans keep on with routine.

11   April, 1945   **120**

Word of death of Roosevelt—Germans simply announce, make no comment—Germans using some prisoners for farm work—These trade with us for food they steal—Bob Jensen, also out of my train-

Table of Contents

ing class, appears—Meet many Australians, New Zealanders, others in mixing of various camps—April 29, 1945! for us, war's over!!! Tanks reach us, liberate camp

12 May, 1945   **128**

Souvenir hunters have field day—We are moved out to Ingolstadt, on Danube. Leave from there by plane for France (Lucky Strike) and final freedom.

Afterword   **133**

Appendices   **134**
1. Further Details about Interrogations.
2. Our Escape Committees, and Work on Escapes.
3. Our Radio Receiver—How It Was Built, How Concealed from German Searches.
4. Tin Can Carpentry—How It Was Done, Improvised Tools, etc.
5. Games for Amusement—Confusing the Guards for Laughs.
6. Character Studies of German Soldiery—How Organized, How Obeyed
7. Some Scenes from Camps—How Senegalese Cursed Out Guards, etc.

Index   **150**

Foreword

An explanation is needed as a foreword—an explanation for the almost total omission (except as "Appendices" near the very end) of another aspect of our lives as prisoners:

Of course we were constantly trying to figure out ways to escape—an effort that occupied the almost full-time attention of a "committee" (which had to be especially careful for security reasons), preparation of dried foods as best we could for survival, the digging of a number of quite elaborate tunnels and such things. (See Appendix #2.) And, of course, we had our own radio—a crystal set put together by some genius among us, which the Germans never found; how we managed to get some information "out" of the camp, by slipping notes and things into the luggage of Red Cross and other emissaries. (See Appendix #3.)

I had a very good reason for omitting this sort of thing:

This diary was kept in small notebooks, on scraps of paper or whatever was available, written in pencil or ink—whatever came to hand—largely as an exercise in something to do.

But our German "hosts" were extremely nervous about all this (if, for example, we had our own radio and thus could receive orders from our own commands, they feared a concerted uprising). So they conducted unannounced and numerous searches of everything and everyone. Thus I was concerned that they might somehow find the diary—and through it, get some key as to what we were doing secretly.

Hence, mention of these matters was carefully omitted. I hinted at it a little, of course, in the notes that start "good news today." The "good news" was of course information that the Allies had won a victory, or—much more important from our viewpoint—were getting closer to us.

EEH

Introduction

It's a strange thing when you go to war: You somehow never expect to be taken prisoner.

You figure (academically, of course) that you might be killed—that's always something to be considered with something of a thrill (even though you really don't believe it). You might be wounded. Or you could come out a hero.

But taken prisoner?

That's a role few men picture for themselves.

Of course, we had lectures on the subject of how to conduct ourselves if we fell into enemy hands. And we listened respectfully.

But we listened with the same feeling we'd had when our parents told us what would happen if we weren't good. Of course, we were going to be good, so there wasn't any reality in the dire punishment promised.

And, of course, we weren't going to be taken prisoner.

◆ ◆ ◆

However, to get into this diary:

After a couple of years of individual and crew training, we were assigned to our outfit in England as a replacement crew, ready for combat.

Which brings me—rather suddenly, I'll admit—to June 29, 1944, the day we finished our active participation in this part of the war, anyway, by getting ourselves shot down. So I've started the day-to-day diary on that date, since that was also our first day as prisoners of war.

First, though, I ought to list the crew—again, as much for my own benefit as any other.

We were: Robert E. Cole, of Rochester, New York, pilot; Robert B. Post, of Pendleton, Indiana, co-pilot; myself, navigator; David L. Smart, Jr., of Kansas City, Missouri, bombardier—all of us being second lieutenants. The rest of the crew were: S/Sgt. J. F. Santora, Jr., San Jose, California, radioman; S/Sgt. J. D. Sorenson, Waukesha, Wisconsin, engineer; S/Sgt. John Currie, Scranton, Pennsylvania, crew chief; Sgts. W. K. Leonard, J. J. Moos and F. A. Hart, Jr., gunners. We were pretty well mixed as to age, background and origin: Cole and I, nudging 28, the oldest; Post 25, Smart 20. The enlisted men's ages ranged from 19 to 24.

And so —— ——.

Chapter 1

♦

June, 1944

June 29, 1944
England (Halesworth)

My watch showed 4 A.M. this cold, dank morning, when the Sergeant came banging on our Nissen-Hut door to wake us up for the mission.

Four in the morning. But this was "double British War Time", so it was really 2 A.M. local time. And it was, as usual, cold and wet outside—and this was a strange country and we were a long way from home.

But we got up—Army experience had taught us long since that when you have to get up there's no remedy but to do so, and right now. So we fumbled in the darkness for shoes and pants and caps (blackout in force—no lights to be shown), and then blundered outside to find the latrine for an attempt to wash out that fuzzy feeling.

And then, hurriedly buckling on our .45's (all officers will go armed at all times) we groped our way, single file, down a pitch-black road to a mess hall.

Bob Cole, pilot, strode first as befitted the crew commander; then Bob Post, co-pilot; then I, as navigator, and Dave Smart, bombardier.

♦ ♦ ♦

We'd come a long way—the four of us and our six enlisted crewmen—for this moment.

Cole, lean and tough, left a machine operator's job at Rochester, N.Y.: short, slim, quiet Post left his production work at Anderson, Indiana; stocky, sturdy Smart came fresh from engineering school in Kansas, and I from the newspaperman's world of New York.

Through buck-private, basic training, to cadet examinations, to flying schools, to transition training, to "phases", and finally to the long jump—as a crew and in our own plane—across the North Atlantic to England. And to War.

♦ ♦ ♦

Breakfast was hasty, and we talked rapidly and made feeble jokes about condemned men and hearty breakfasts, and somehow the powdered eggs and the greenish coffee didn't sit too well; and then we left by truck for the briefing room, still a mile away.

The Wrong Side of the Fence

That briefing was just as dramatic as they always were—partly, I think, because they were meant to be, and partly because of our own feelings. I can't quite vouch for the others, but I know I was busy—between feverish periods of work—sorting out a lot of jumbled thoughts having to do with the possibilities of not getting back.

We filed into the big briefing room—an oversized Nissen really—and stood at attention while the colonel came in and the chaplain prayed for us. The big map on the wall was veiled—and there was a deep gasp as the intelligence officer pulled back the cloth to show a bold red line plunging straight across Germany—nearly 600 miles in—and then began to drone his reports of flak concentrations, possible fighter opposition and other facts of our wartime life.

We took our notes solemnly; broke up for individual briefings (Cole and Post to get recognition signals, formation data, emergency procedure; Dave to get aiming points and release points; I to plot courses, note predicted winds and weather, coordinates of aiming points, check points, flak areas; the crew to see that the ship was in shape, bombs armed, guns loaded, gas aboard) and then rushed for the quartermaster—where we found we couldn't all get complete electrically-heated flying suits (I got only a jacket and boots)—and then a jeep trip to the plane.

There were only minutes to spare, so we crouched under the ugly wing of our B-24 and I got out the maps to show the crew where we were headed, give them some idea of what to look for. The motors began to snort along the hardstands, we climbed into our cramped takeoff positions, and were ready to go.

What does a man think about when he goes to battle like that? I really don't know.

I remember coming up (to myself, fortunately) with a couple of deathless thoughts like "Well, this is IT!", but for the most part it was a jumble and I was too busy for coherent thought along those lines.

Scared? Sure. But the discipline that had been drilled into us for a couple of years or more held tightly on our nerves, and kept all of us at the jobs that would take us to danger.

◆ ◆ ◆

I've never seen a thousand planes going by in one mass, from the ground. It must be an impressive sight. But it can't be more impressive than the view from an airplane in the middle of such a formation.

The navigator has a good seat to watch from, up in the plexi-glass-enclosed nose of a B-24, and so I watched the legions gather.

From all over the sky, from every point of the compass it seemed to me, they rose above the soft billowing white clouds that covered England. Tens and twenties and hundreds of airplanes—great, lumbering, blunt-nosed things, ugly in their war paint—purposeful and somehow individually alive—arranging themselves in mathematical formations, rank on rank, and drowning the noises of our own engines in the roar of millions of horsepower.

June, 1944

A B-24 is ugly enough on the ground, but in the air it looks downright vicious. And each of these had 8,000 pounds of sudden death in its belly.

This was a full air division—1,000 planes, eight million pounds of bombs, twenty million rounds of machine-gun ammunition, three million gallons of gasoline, ten thousand men—all headed to destroy three small enemy cities and the war-making potential that was in them. Nothing like the "coal runs" we'd already made—picking up bomb loads, flying maybe 20 minutes to France, dumping them to help troops on the ground, going back for more.

Such a tremendous show of power is somehow incomprehensible even when you see it—and it ran through my head that someone really ought to warn the people down below of what was coming.

◆ ◆ ◆

While we were training, I often cursed the complexities of the navigator's job—the endless figuring, the constant note-taking, the ceaseless checks on instruments, reports to the pilot, checks on oxygen and the rest that go to give the navigator the earned title of "flying bookkeeper".

But I was glad enough for the work this day. I had no gun to handle, but my weather notes, observations, checks on ground objects and courses, and other minutiae kept me occupied until we got on target and Dave took over to fulfill the object of the flight.

Implacable as death itself and seemingly as impervious, our sky-filling armada swung into its bombing run, brushing through the black puff-balls of flak that bloomed so silently and innocently along its path. Advancing rank on rank on rank it covered the town and the airfield and the factory below, dropping its bomb-loads in curtains each a little ahead of the other, rolling up that town into an ever-growing red blanket that was pierced at intervals with brighter spots of red.

It seemed to be a silent holocaust, under the earth-shaking rumble of our engines—just that growing red blanket so far below us.

But just as Dave said the traditional—"Bombs away, let's get the Hell out of here!"; just as we started to wheel into a sharp turn away from the target and toward home—we staggered. Through the plexiglass on my right I could see our outboard engine suddenly windmill crazily, gas and oil streaming from it, splashing on the fuselage.

Things happened quickly—an unintelligible intercom conversation between Cole, Post and the engineer; our immediate loss of position in the formation; the suddenly menacing appearance of the flak clouds; an uneven rhythm in the thrumming of the engines; my sudden realization that there were 600 miles to go toward "home" and that we'd have to make it alone—on Cole's skill as pilot, on mine as navigator, on the crewmen who knew their jobs.

It was a tight spot, and though we were at 28,000 feet and it was 40 below zero, we were sweating heavily. We knew we couldn't afford to be hit by anything—flak or incandescent fighter-plane "tracer" bullets. Not with gallons of highly volatile gasoline spraying over us.

The Wrong Side of the Fence

And we couldn't stop the escape of the gas. The plane was bleeding to death. And in back of our minds the thought began to grow—we might have to jump. None of us had jumped, ever, though we'd all had lectures on it. But to jump into hostile country—to jump at all from five miles up—was a heart-stopping thought in itself.

We began to throw things out to help the plane along; we tried to pump the gas out of the injured tank; we tried everything we knew. And we all—gunners, pilot, navigator, bombardier—sweated and cursed and figured and worried along somehow, 500 miles or more.

All across Germany, smiling and green but sinister below us, over the Dutch border, over the Zuyder Zee, to the seacoast, we managed to cripple her along, and England was only 100 miles away.

But it couldn't be done.

As we came over the North Sea coast, Cole called me to say we had maybe 150 gallons of gas left (the sight gauges were not always reliable), we were losing altitude at 200 feet per minute, would lose another engine soon (we did, almost immediately)—and how about a radius-of-action problem? Could we make it home?

There was a 40-mile headwind—and I never want to do a problem like that again. I had to report it couldn't be done. We couldn't get home. Cole didn't hesitate—the crew commander is responsible for the lives of his men.

We swung back in a great arc—back from the sea and England, back to the Dutch coast, and to an order we didn't want to hear.

It didn't come as it would in story books. No dramatic, tense words.

Only Cole's voice sounding strange in the intercom:

"We'll have to get rid of this kid. Get ready to walk .... Luck ...."

Dave climbed clumsily out of the nose-turret where he'd been riding, freeing himself of a web of wires and hoses, and I know my face was as white as his.

We couldn't say anything—there wasn't time, we couldn't hear, and there wasn't anything to say. We kicked his bombsight to pieces, he helped me fasten my chute straps. We exchanged a look and a handshake, and he disappeared down the knee-high tunnel that led to the bomb bays.

I had a minute more—just long enough to try to give the crew an idea of where we were and what direction to take to head for Normandy where the nearest help was—before the intercom went out completely and the men began to jump.

I crouched under my navigation table and pulled the red "emergency handle" and the nose-wheel doors flopped suddenly open and I was looking straight down—17,500 feet down, to be exact.

If I was sweating before, it was worse now. I didn't want to jump, didn't want to leave the plane which suddenly seemed warm and alive—and safe—to me.

June, 1944

Suddenly, the bodies of the crew members flashed past my hole in the ship—twisting and turning grotesquely like rag dolls falling. I counted six, seven—that was Dave—and before I had a chance to get any scareder, I somersaulted down and out.

There was a tremendous, breath-taking rush and buffeting in the slip stream, and I can't recall anything but sensations, and then I was out of it and falling.

But it didn't seem like falling at all.

The air seemed almost solid—like water—and I found to my considerable delight that I could actually fly. No, I don't mean that exactly, but I could turn over on my back or on my face quite easily—as though I were swimming. I did that—once to look for the plane, plummeting crazily far off toward the sea, and once to look for the chutes.

And I wasn't scared at all. Even remembered I'd left my watch strapped to my "G" box. And my wallet, with its pictures of Ann.

Quite consciously, I figured out that I'd fallen about 10,000 feet, and thought it about time to open my chute, turned on my back, reached for the rip-cord and pulled it. And felt kind of foolish as the thing came away in my hand. I knew it should, but I wasn't happy about it at the moment.

But the silk opened with a vicious crack, and an impossible, agonizing jerk. I seemed to stop short in the air and things got a little dizzy for a moment.

The leg and arm straps exerted a painful pressure, particularly in the groin, but I found I was unable to relieve it. I couldn't manage to shift, somehow.

I hadn't realized I wasn't hearing anything but the rush of air before—but now everything was suddenly very quiet.

An odd thing. I seemed to hang, swaying over so gently, completely detached from the world. Down here it was warm—a fine June day, and Holland was spread out like a big picture book below, the canals making geometrical patterns in the checkered landscape, smoke rising lazily here and there.

I seemed to sit there for an endless stretch of time—and the four great silk blossoms that were holding others of the crew below me maintained their positions, and I began to wonder if I'd ever get down.

But it seemed best to spot hazards on the ground, and I began to look around, and the ground seemed suddenly to be coming up at me at an alarming rate. Like one of those movies that you see purporting to be taken from the car in which the robber is fleeing, trees began to spring out of the ground and rise up to me, houses, cattle, fields, canals appeared and grew larger—and I had time only to grab the shroud lines to relax my legs and I hit the ground.

I mean I hit. Bet they heard that fall in Amsterdam.

I lit on my rear end and flipped over on my back and banged myself on the back of the head—and although somewhat goofy, all I could think of was that I was down—this was the ground. The good earth. And it wasn't moving away from me. The ground! Never felt so sincerely attached to it before, even though something had gone wrong with my back when I arched over backward as I hit.

The Wrong Side of the Fence

There was a cow off in the corner of the field—and it didn't even bother to look up. Kept right on chewing as if this sort of thing went on every day.

I was partially "out" for perhaps a half-minute, it seemed to me, just luxuriating in the feeling of being safe on the ground. And then a peculiar rushing sound was around me, and I looked up and there were Dutch men and women—wooden shoes and all—on all sides.

Kindly people they were, and obviously sympathetic and willing to help. A boy in the group could speak English—he asked me if I was hurt. I told him I didn't know—I really thought I'd broken my back—but that I'd try to stand up and see.

They helped me up—and I began to collect enough sense to realize that this was no place for me to be standing passing the time of day. So I asked the lad if he'd seen any Germans about. He gestured silently and I turned around—and there was a little bit of a German soldier, standing cautiously about 30 feet away, but with a machine-pistol in his hand.

There was no doubt of the target of that weapon—and I'd seen a small tree cut down with one.

It was most undramatic—even stereotyped to the point of a German officer rushing up to me to tell me, in French, that "for me, the war is over". I had become a prisoner of war.

The German officer was a little man—like his private with the gun, in fact like most Europeans I'd seen so far.

A little man with bad teeth and thick glasses and an ill-fitting grey fatigue uniform—but a confident, bustling little man, none the less. Taking advantage of my state as a prisoner, he searched me—looking first for weapons, but then for smokes. He found a full pack of cigarettes in my pocket with a satisfied grunt, grabbed one cigarette to smoke hungrily, put the rest in his pants. Didn't offer me one.

Then, talking volubly in what he evidently thought was French (he saw I had understood his "Pour vous, la guerre est fini") he led me at a fast walk across the fields to a truck standing by the roadside.

It was odd. I strode along behind him in my big, clumsy flying boots, my back killing me, dragging my parachute after me, looking at the people around the field and trying to smile at them. But it didn't seem to be me at all. It was as if I was watching the whole thing from a theater seat somewhere.

It just wasn't real, couldn't be.

In this sort of dream-state, I climbed into the back of the truck—helped by a very young German private—and did what I could about getting comfortable on the floor. They insisted that I sit there, so only my head appeared above the tail-gate.

The truck started, and bounced horribly along the road between two ditches. I became sure my back was broken—I could feel the bones jarring every time we hit a bump.

June, 1944

The truck travels perhaps two blocks and stops, and I watch Jack Currie, our master gunner, climb aboard. And then, beside a quaint little house, we find Smart and Joe Santora, our radioman, both in bad shape. Joe has a broken leg, and there was something wrong with Dave's feet—he could hardly walk. I get out, though, and with his help, managed to get Santora into the truck. The Germans watch, but make no move to help.

And then in quick succession, we picked up the others—Post, Jim Leonard, gunner; Jack Sorenson, engineer. No sign of Cole, Jim Moos or Frank Hart—two other gunners.

I've never been sure just what the Germans were trying to do—show us off as prizes, or actually trying to find the others—but they rode us around and around that little town for nearly an hour—going up one road and down another, around a big square of fields and houses.

Once we stopped at a substantial, thatch-roofed farmhouse, and the German lieutenant jumped importantly off, followed by two of his men. They bustled purposefully behind the house, and we heard one shot. And then they came back, carrying a parachute.

Still don't quite see what they were trying to prove. Somehow, none of us believed they'd actually shot anybody.

Finally they got tired of the merry-go-round, and we started off in a southeasterly direction. The Dutch residents, who showed no particular fear of the Germans, crowded near the truck—giving us the "V" sign, smiling, making every effort to show they were friends, and had no part in this.

The countryside continued my illusion of a theater. It looked so much like picture-book Holland that I expected to find somebody shifting scenes any time. The thatched roofs, the sturdy brick houses and fat barns, the wooden shoes, the windmills—were all there.

But the ride was painful for me—for all of us. We were all banged up somehow—I with my bad back, Dave and Joe with their bad legs, Post with a sprained shoulder, Currie nursing a very sore head where (it developed later) his captor had slugged him with a rifle-butt; Sorenson with a bad leg.

And every time the truck hit a bump, it was agony for me. One of the guards—the same young boy who helped in my initial capture, finally took to warning us when we were coming to a bump—and we braced ourselves as best we could to take the shock.

They took us to a town called Hoorn, near the Zuyder Zee—a pretty place and a fairly sizeable one from what we saw of it. In front of what must have once been the town hall, just off a pretty square, we were told to get out, and go inside.

Dave, hardly able to move but refusing to be carried, moving like an automaton and unable to bend his knees, managed somehow to get up four steps and stagger into a great room that looked as if it might be the mayor's office. Here they let us sit down—on the floor—under guard, while they inventoried what they'd taken from us.

The Wrong Side of the Fence

We were all in pretty good physical condition when this day started ten hours before. But we were exhausted now, emotionally and physically, and were happy enough just to sit quietly. I found it more comfortable to lie flat on the floor—as did Dave and Santora.

Shortly, a German major arrived. Since I was the only one wearing insignia, he addressed a rapid series of questions at me through one of his men who spoke a classroom English—and got no results, I think.

His face got redder and redder as he went on, and he finally ended by dropping his monocle and bawling me out roundly for not standing in his presence.

Funny, it never occurred to me that he really had the upper hand. I was just awfully comfortable on the floor, and didn't feel like getting up at all.

He went away, finally, very red of face and muttering under his breath—but he apparently issued some orders that we'd wanted: Post and I had been protesting loudly (in English) of our need for medical attention, and finally two German medical orderlies came in to look at Smart and Santora.

They said neither man had a broken bone (an obvious falsehood), but they did at least put a splint on Joe's leg and tie up one of Dave's feet, so that we could move them a little more easily.

With that, the Germans apparently finished whatever it was they had to do at Hoorn, and they loaded us on another truck—a much smaller one, like those half-ton pickups the grocer uses at home—and in it took us some 30 kilometers (the signs said) to a place called Alkmaar, where there was an airfield.

A ragged, banged-up group we must have looked as we dismounted there, carrying Dave and Santora, to the side of what looked to have been some businessman's modest country place. They had us sit down under a tree, ringed us with guards—and introduced us to Jim Moos, who was a sight.

A big, rangy boy, he'd gotten away for an hour or so, and managed to obtain some civilian clothing far too small for him. His arms and legs stuck out of them scarecrow-fashion, and he looked sheepish enough for having been caught.

All this, you understand, had the same queer, dreamlike quality I began to feel earlier. It couldn't be me—couldn't be our crew, sprawled exhaustedly under the trees, ragged and dirty, surrounded by the badly-dressed, runty German soldiery.

But of course, it was.

One by one they had us go into the house, where a bespectacled sergeant took our pedigrees—and our watches, insignia, wings, knives and any other valuables. Very methodical they were, insisting that each man witness the procedure.

Even Dave—who was unable to walk at all now—and Santora had to be carried into the house to witness this formality.

June, 1944

This over, we made our very painful way—pushing the two cripples in a wheelbarrow—to another house, long disused. In what had been "the front room" we found eight very dirty straw pallets.

Here the Germans posted guards, and as we looked around in the semi-darkness, Cole and Leonard walked in.

They had landed close together and unhurt in a wheat field. Unable to move because of the flatness of the country, they'd planned to wait for nightfall, then try moving. But they were seen and caught before they had a chance.

It was a bad night.

The straw sacks were placed side-by-side and very close together, and the Germans insisted we sleep that way. None of us was nearly comfortable. I lay between Santora and Dave—and found that my back wouldn't let me lie in one position long. But every time I moved, no matter how carefully, I feared jarring one of the injured men.

Oh yes—we had "food". One thick, almost unchewable slice of black bread which seems to be made of large amounts of sawdust and little else, and a mug of what the Germans insisted was coffee. It was awful, but we hadn't eaten since 1 A.M. of the previous day, so we managed to get it down.

June 30, 1944
Alkmaar, Holland

They dug us out of an exhausted sleep at 7 A.M.—all of us beginning to feel very dirty and disheveled, since we'd had no opportunity to wash or shave.

"Breakfast" consists of another slice of black bread—with jam—and more "coffee", which is terrible to our taste, but hot. Pretty thin fare for men used to three heavy and varied meals per day. But we are hungry, and heed Cole's advice to eat everything possible, since we might not get more.

Then, accompanied by six guards—all of them apparently men of 35 or more, all of them uniformly sloppy in dirty grey uniforms—we make our painful way to a producer-gas truck, load the injured men as gently as we can, and are driven to a railroad station.

It's a big station, with two platforms and four tracks for electric trains. Seems very heavily travelled, crowds reminiscent of a Westchester suburban station, pour into and out of trains, mill around the platforms. We are right in the middle of the southbound platform, and are surrounded by and stared at in a most friendly fashion by the crowds. We are well guarded, however, no room to do anything towards escape.

A train pulls in and the guards clear a third class compartment for themselves and us. And we travel through Amsterdam, Utrecht, Maastricht and other towns I don't remember to Eindhoven, where we get off to await another train in the waiting room of the station. Country from Amsterdam east is flooded about a foot deep in water, both sides of the railway embankment.

We've had nothing to smoke for two days now, and it's beginning to tell on us. In the station, it seems everyone is smoking. It begins to be nerve-

The Wrong Side of the Fence

wracking to watch. People come drifting into the station, sit at tables (it's also a sort of restaurant), open their briefcases, take out their lunches and eat in almost complete silence. And they smoke incessantly.

Our guards do the same, finally breaking out a bit of black bread for us—bread and nothing more. Finally, a Dutch waiter asks permission of the guards, and brings us "coffee".

Santora is in great pain with his leg, and finally the German sergeant in charge of our guards gives him a cigarette. Joe smokes it down to where he'd ordinarily throw it away, then passes it on to us. We each take a puff, finally getting it down to the last few grains. I have never seen such a complete job of smoking in my life. We've noticed the Germans doing the same—smoking down until the lips burn, then putting the stub in a holder and finishing it. By our standards, the tobacco is very bad, but the smoke tastes good.

Dave, who doesn't smoke, is having a rough time too—his feet must pain him terribly, and since he's the one who's always been the most active of us all, he must hate to be so helpless now. But he keeps quiet about it. I believe I'm making more noise about my back—which is painful enough—than he does about his condition.

Finally, our train arrives, and we get aboard, the guards assuring us we will get real medical attention for Dave and Joe in about an hour.

We ride to Venlo. This is obviously a border town. We are taken into what had been a customs station, and watch engines puffing by carrying the legend "Deutsche Reichsbahn". Here, also we meet members of another of our crews—they had crash-landed and it was their plane we saw burning in the field yesterday.

The task of carrying Dave and Joe is becoming painful for us, as well as for them. And poor Joe now has to use the toilet. Cole and I carry him there—an awful job.

But we are forced to pile the two, and both crews, into a bus—along with a lot of soldiery—and are taken quite a long ways through the factory town to a very large building that seemed to have been a factory. We carry Dave and Joe to the foot of a long flight of stairs, where we leave them—Dave sitting disconsolately on the third step, unable to move, in pain, and hating to see us go; Joe on a stretcher, eyes closed, saying "so long".

We've never seen them again. They were taken to a hospital for treatment, we were told. We'll have to pick up their story after this is over, I guess.

We others climb three flights of stairs, are searched again, and then put into single rooms, alone—our first taste of solitary confinement.

The rooms are small—maybe eight by ten—with one glazed window, blocked by columns of brick serving as bars. Furniture is a rough table, bench, and a wooden double-decker bed, complete with wood slats and burlap bags filled with wood shavings for mattresses. They are rock-hard. No blankets.

Dull enough. But they bring us more black bread, with some kind of syrup on it, and "coffee". We are exhausted, and sleep like the dead, sprains and discomfort and all.

Chapter 2

◆

July, 1944

July 1, 1944
Venlo, Holland

No prospect of getting out of here. In fact, no prospect of anything. No one has talked to us at all, about anything. Except the guard, who doesn't profess to speak English beyond the words "toilet" and "water".

This is deadly. Nothing to do but sit on the bunk and stare at the walls. Can't get my head through the brick columns on the window—and the glass is painted so I couldn't see out anyway, even if I could get close.

Occasionally, I can hear the others in the hallway, going to the toilet, with the guard. And Moos singing "Basin Street Blues"—he's a jive fan. And the incessant pacing of the guard's boots on the wooden hallway floor. Maddening not to be able to talk to those fellows, or understand what they say to each other.

No shave for three days now—I'm growing quite a brush. No washing either. Feel very dirty and disreputable. No smokes, either.

Nothing to do. Nothing at all to do. No place to go. Nothing to see. Never realized what poor company I am for myself. Wonder whether Ann and the folks have been notified that I'm missing yet. Must be rough on them. Wish I could let them know.

Go over and over the mission. Did I make any mistakes? Could we have made it back? Why didn't I delay my jump more? Wonder if Dave's being taken care of? Who'd ever thought, three months ago, that I'd be in this spot? First chance I've had to think much.

But wait. I'm getting myself in the dumps. That way lies madness.

Nothing to do. Better not think at all. Soup and potatoes for lunch—first hot meal.

Better sleep. Doesn't take thinking.

The Wrong Side of the Fence

July 2, 1944
Venlo, Holland

Got us up at 7 A.M. this morning (I asked the guard for the time), gave us a slice of black bread, no chance to shave or wash, bundled us into the bus and back to the station aboard a train again.

New set of guards, led by a lieutenant now—a pudgy blond fellow with a cleft chin who thinks a good deal of himself and his looks. And including a sergeant who speaks some English. He says Dave and Joe are being cared for in a hospital, ends his remarks with an order to "shut up".

It's a pleasure to be out of that room—to see the others.

So, via third-class again, to Cologne, where we get off to await another train.

The city is shockingly damaged—regular swath cut through its middle. The Cathedral, which we can see, since the depot no longer has a roof, towers seemingly untouched, except for broken windows.

This is our first experience with a crowd in hostile country, and we are uneasy about it. But except for a very few, most of them women who plainly hated us, we saw little evidence of hostility. Just curiosity—nothing more.

There's a trainload of kids in brown shirts on the station platform. They sing "Deutschland Uber Alles", wave little daggers and swastika flags as we go by. Most of them seem to need a good pants paddling more than anything else.

We are paraded through the station by our lieutenant—who seems very conscious of his impression on the local ladies—and down a long flight of stairs to a great dungeon-like cavity under the streets. It obviously had been a wine cellar, and as obviously an air-raid shelter. Damp and cold, but here we remain for two hours, while the guards feed us another slice of black bread, and water.

Then back upstairs and on another train for a long grind this time—to Frankfurt-Am-Main, they tell us.

Under other circumstances, this trip would be pleasant enough, I guess. The countryside is really beautiful, as the train runs parallel to the Rhine for miles. There's heavy shipping on the river in fast, long, canal-boat-like steamers. The grape arbors climb the hills, and we can see old castles and watchtowers on the heights.

But we're prisoners, can't show ourselves at the windows in stations.

Here and there along the way, while we're on sidings and suchlike, we see Russian prisoners. They seem cheerful, give us the high-sign.

So, through Bingen and Coblenz to Frankfurt—which was a shambles, worse than Cologne. The huge railroad station had no roof and little else but tracks, but trains were running. Here too, we encountered curious, but not openly hostile, crowds.

They take us to a dank cellar—little more than a hole, where we wait an hour for another train. Thence, by a roundabout route to a suburb north of the

July, 1944

city—Oberursel by name. Here an interurban trolley is supposed to take us to our destination—Dulag Luft, the place of interrogation.

But there is no trolley, and so we have to walk. Our Lieutenant doesn't like the prospect, it's a warm day. But to some of us it is a lot worse. Post, for instance, has no shoes—only big flying boots that slither around on his feet.

But there's nothing to do but to walk, and we do—a mile or more through a pleasant suburban town, with factories stuck here and there among the trees.

Until we reach a gate in a barbed-wire fence and were admitted, to face a group of unpainted wooden German army buildings.

After some preliminaries, we enter the building. I should describe this—spent a lot of time in it. It was a one-story wooden thing, built along a long hallway—maybe 300 feet long, and branching off into five cells, labelled A, B, C, D and E corridors, all branching off to the south of the hallway.

"E" corridor contained a few offices, and then, like all the others, was lined with small cells. There were 33 cells, each 8 x 10, in each corridor. The rooms were finished with something that looked like sugar-cane board, once painted white. Otherwise, the furniture was the same as at Venlo.

We are assigned rooms quickly, and locked in. More black bread and a really awful concoction that they call tea, and which I couldn't drink at all. That is supper.

Then the lights go out, and a mouse starts gnawing somewhere in the room. First night.

July 3, 1944
Oberursel, Germany

This is real solitary. This morning after breakfast—black bread and that horrible "tea"—they took me to see a German sergeant, who asked me a lot of questions which I refused to answer, and then told me more about the squadron than I knew myself. It was really amazing, the amount of information he had! names and dates and places.

I remained non-committal, and he seemed mad and the interview ended. Then they "mugged" me—beard and all—and returned me to my cell.

And then, as the English say, "I'd had it."

Again. Nothing to do. No place to go. Nothing to see. No one to talk to. But I've had a taste of this before. Knew the danger of thinking, just sitting.

Discover that my window has a transom which had been carefully blocked with a wooden screen to prevent looking out. But the wooden block is broken on one side, and by standing on the table, it gives me a view of the corner of the yard outside—of a place where a guard paces incessantly, a corner of an office building across the way where personnel and occasionally a prisoner and guard walk by. Whiled away an hour looking out.

Then I discover that the burlap bag that forms my mattress is very poorly woven, can be unraveled a string at a time, very slowly, to produce a creditable

The Wrong Side of the Fence

length of twine. No use for twine, but something to do. An hour or so could go that way.

And I've had no chance to clean my teeth. And since my mattress was filled with wood shavings, I've got toothpicks to hand. What with cleaning my fingernails with my belt buckle and my teeth with the shavings, I put in another hour.

And then there's the mouse. I got feeding him (or her) with a little of the black bread crust, which I can't eat, finally get him to be less afraid of me.

These things, plus time out for eating, going to the toilet, take up the time.

Silly business for a grown man? But there isn't anything at all to do. And I've got to keep doing something, anything, to keep from thinking.

Found later, that Cole had whiled away the time by figuring out how big his room was, and how many times he'd have to go around the open space to make a mile walk—and then walked it daily. And Squadron Leader Cole—a Britisher we met later—spent the whole day manufacturing a brush set out of woodshavings and using it to clean out an old bottle in his room.

Tonight I heard them call out Post, Currie, Sorenson—they're leaving, I gather through the door. Am I the only one left? Heard them call out Moos and Leonard this morning. No sign of Cole, though.

Well, another day with no bath, no shave, no smokes.

July 4, 1944
Oberursel, Germany

There are nineteen studs in the door of this room (No. 26), one of them with a head broken in two. And 22 studs in the ceiling, arranged in four rows of five each, with two extra around the light fixture. There's a sign, neatly typewritten, pasted on the door, which says that "Writing on any place in this room is strictly forbidden, and any infraction will be punished under the regulations." Wonder what the regulations are. But the walls are full of initials and dates—some of them way back in '43.

Fourth of July—Independence Day. A fine way to celebrate. In prison. Wonder what they're doing at home. Do they know I'm safe? Ann was in Illinois when I last heard from her—does she know? Hold it, chum. Hold it.

There's a clock somewhere around, with chimes. So I can tell the hour. At 11 o'clock they got me out—take me unshaven and dirty across the street.

I'm brought into the office of a German captain—a short, fat man, bald as an egg, with heavy horn-rimmed goggles and a mustache to give his blank face character. He's maybe 50 years old.

His office is a big, bare room, overlooking the prison building, furnished with a big desk, a couple of chairs—and the walls lined with maps of Europe. They're English maps, not German. On the desk is a copy of *Esquire* (for April, 1941), a *Time* equally old.

He greets me by name, dismisses the guard, gives me a cigarette and lights it for me. It tastes good.

July, 1944

Humming a bit, he gets up, goes to the map, marks our base on it. He turns to me, asks if that's correct. When I don't answer, he takes almost childlike pleasure in giving me the details—and more—that the sergeant gave me yesterday.

He knows I was the navigator, and he wants me to outline our course. I keep my answers polite, but tell him nothing. I keep taking cigarettes from his pack—which he's left incautiously on the desk—and he shows annoyance. He asks me what I am fighting for—I tell him because I want to go home. He says that we and the British and the Germans should be fighting together against the Russians. I make no answer.

He gets up suddenly, says I am being silly—that I'll have to spend a couple of more days in solitary if I don't cooperate. I tell him that's his decision to make. Almost eagerly, he asks if I want to see him again? I tell him that's his province, not mine.

He calls the guard, and back I go to my coverlet-picking and mouse feeding.

At 6 P.M., from the window-crack, I see Cole crossing to the interrogation building. So he's still here.

July 5, 1944
Oberursel, Germany

This day starts out like the others. Up at 7 A.M., by the clock chimes (wonder where the damned thing is), out to use the toilet. I've found that there is a water tap in the toilet room, and by using it when the guard isn't looking, I can do something towards washing my hands at least. Nothing like soap and water, but some attempt at cleaning myself up, anyway.

And so back to my coverlet-picking and window watching and mouse feeding. My golly, how the day drags. Seems as if the captain was really sore and meant it about my staying here.

Only ten o'clock.

I can hear the guy in room 24 (next to me on the left) walking around and around and around. We've discovered we can talk a bit by putting our heads close to the mutual wall that separates our cells. He's a sergeant, been here ten days already, he tells me. I don't blame him for hiking, but he's been driving me nuts. Fellow in 28, on the other side, calls in to say good morning, and how am I making it. He's a pilot—also in five days.

Eleven o'clock. I hear the guards clomping down the hall—never saw such an army as the Germans to make noise with their feet—they stop at my cell. It seems the captain wants to see me again. Oh well, he won't get much. And I should get another cigarette or two.

In his office, the captain is gruff today. And smarter. He doesn't offer me the pack of cigarettes, only one, this time. He waves me to his wall—and on his maps he has a course plotted with yellow string on a bunch of pins. He asks me if this was our course the other day, but seems to expect no answer from me—which is exactly what he gets. But he's got it pretty close, at that.

The Wrong Side of the Fence

He says no more, goes to his phone, calls for a guard. This is too much for me, and I ask him what goes on. He says I will leave tonight or tomorrow morning. Cole will leave with me. No reason for the sudden change—I can't see what he's learned any more from me now than he got yesterday. But this is no time to argue. He gives me a note, saying I'm entitled to a shave, a book, and a wash. That's plenty for me. (See Appendix #1.)

Back at my cell I get a book—a mystery story. Lunch—potato soup—is being served and it tastes good. But first I'm given a basin, a razor with a nicked blade, some soap—and I get my first look at myself in a mirror—complete with an inch of beard.

At home, Ann would never approve of my growing a mustache. I can see now why. I hack it off, roughly and quite painfully, but off. And then strip down in the washroom and clean up. Even this makes me feel like a million dollars. And I feel I look more like a human being right now than I have in a week.

In the cell again. 24 and 28 sound wistful when I tell them I'm leaving, and they tell me their names and say we'll get together sometime. But it's silly and we know it. I've never seen them, have no idea what they look like.

I devour the book in two hours, get another, read that, and am well into a third when they call me out again—this time to move, since we're being taken to another barracks in the camp to spend the night and will move on to another camp in the morning, the guards say.

Out in the hall, they line us up and return some of our belongings to us—my watch and my cigarette lighter (which is dry and no use to me), but they keep my knife. It's a real pleasure to have a watch again, though. To be able to tell the time, any time I want to know it, gives me a great bang, for some reason. Silly, too, since I'm not going anyplace and time means little to me now.

We're a motley crew in the hall—an American major in a flying suit with his oak-leaf on his cap, a British squadron commander, a couple of other British officers, a bunch of enlisted men. But we're all pleased as kids just to be seeing another human being again, just to be talking to someone again. Cole joins in, looking thin but pleased. It's good to see him.

They line us up, march us out the door and to the end of the camp surrounding the prison building, where there is a row of barracks, furnished as usual with wood beds and straw mattresses, but in which we are free to move around, talk to each other.

And I finally find the clock. It's atop a picturesque old building up on a hill above us—a building that seems to have been a resort hotel of some kind.

So we spend half the night talking, retelling our adventures at Dulag (interrogation camp) and elsewhere, and finally get to sleep.

It's been an eventful day for us.

July 6, 1944
Oberursel, Germany

We were rousted out at 6 A.M. today and given breakfast—more black bread and that awful "tea". And then cleaned up the barracks, and lined up outside for a roll call.

One of the German sergeants who spoke a precise, schoolbook English, read off our names and some provision of the Geneva Convention covering shipments of this kind. Then Major Hackett (also a prisoner) who, as senior man, is to be in charge of us, read us a form in which we gave parole not to escape during the trip, and—when we approved by voice vote—he signed it for all concerned.

And we're off—the men with bad legs, etc., getting a ride on the trolley, and we making the long hike back through town. Most of us are weaker than we had thought—the walk is very tiring.

At the railroad station we are issued two cigarettes each—though we're told not to smoke them while we are in the station, in sight of German civilians. We'd been without tobacco this long, we can stand it a little longer.

The train finally arrives and we file aboard—third class carriages again. There's a woman conductor, in a clumsy looking approximation of the male railroaders' red and blue uniform. Everybody's first move is to light the cigarette, which are German, but withal, tobacco, and take a deep drag. Cole takes a few drags, then "butts" his, for later use. I follow his example.

In our car, along with us Americans, are three Britishers—the Squadron Leader Cole whom I mentioned before and who is known as "King"; Flight Leftenant David Saunders, and a little Scots gunnery officer, whose broken shoulder has been badly set and gives him endless trouble.

The countryside is really lovely again as we travel northeastward. The sun shines, the fields are green and yellow with crops. Little rivers—here and there with someone bathing in them—wander through the low hills. Carefully planted and tended woodlands are dotted here and there.

The train sort of ambles, but we make progress.

All very well, but we are hungry. So, we fall to discussing favorite dishes—ending (after a particularly luscious description of the preparation of ham-and-sweets) with all of us almost drooling and hungrier than ever.

Finally, after back-switching, waiting on sidings and whatnot, we arrive at Wetzlar, where we are told there is another transient camp. This is a fair-sized town, a manufacturing center, apparently untouched by bombing.

We are marched through the streets and out of the town, and I think again we must be an odd sight. Our guards are so much older than we, and we tower over most of them—they're small men, physically.

The walk is long and tiring, but at the top of a hill about two miles above the town, we enter what looks like a large permanent camp (I learned later it had been a German artillery school). Here we are taken to a large building—and out of a blue sky, addressed by an AMERICAN officer—a first lieutenant

The Wrong Side of the Fence

who introduced himself as Senior American Officer of the camp. He told us we'd be served by a staff of NCO's of our own and the British Army, then left, saying he'd see us later.

Almost forgot to say that as we left the train in town, we spotted two cars with iron bars on them on another track. Our boys were aboard—Moos, Currie, Sorenson, Leonard. We didn't have much chance to say anything, but they shouted that they were OK, that the camp was a good deal, that they were going to a permanent camp.

That's the last we saw of them—there's another story we'll have to pick up later.

Anyway, we are searched again, and then they take away the ratty flying clothes most of the boys have been wearing for so long.

Lord bless the Red Cross! In another room, being dealt out by sergeants who wear insignia we recognize and can understand what we say, are piles of clothes. Not fancy—just plain old G.I. issue, but clean or new. We are issued a G.I. overcoat, trousers (for those who need them), an O.D. shirt, a clean suit of underwear, pair of socks, tooth brushes, toothpaste, razor blades, soap—and two packs of honest-to-God American cigarettes. That's the crowning gift.

They take us to another building where we strip down and take a shower—a hot shower with plenty of soap. I can't quite put into words what that felt like, after wearing the same clothes for 24 hours a day for more than a week, after being unable to wash at all.

Then back into the street—this time in fresh, clean clothes and through another gate, and we're in the camp. And Post is waiting for us—almost, I suspect, with a tear in his eye, and certainly with a catch in his voice. The words "it was good to see him" don't cover the feeling at all. He had been sweating us out since his own arrival here July 4.

With Post as guide, we get a quick look at the camp. It's an enclosure of about an acre and a half, dotted with tents—American tents—in which we are to live; with a cook-house under a long shed.

We, the three Britishers, and five other Americans, commandeer a tent, put our stuff on the straw sacks that will serve as beds, and do one thing in concert.

We light up a real cigarette.

And then it's time for supper.

Thrice blessed be the Red Cross! This is an American supper—made up out of Red Cross parcels. Canned corned-beef, mashed potatoes, butter, bread, a sort of soup. And real coffee—Nescafe—that tastes like coffee. We linger over it.

And then after supper we squat on bricks before out tent, light our cigarettes in luxury, and like rational men we get to discussing the war, and peace, and many things, as the cool of the evening approaches.

It doesn't really take much to satisfy a man. A good meal, good smoke, good talk—a bath. That isn't much to ask of the world.

And so to bed for a real night's rest.

July 7, 1944
Wetzlar, Germany

Up at 7 A.M. of a fine clear morning—a cloudless sky and a bright sun, almost the first clear day we have seen since we've been in Europe. And a decent night's rest, plus clean clothes, a shave and the prospect of a good meal conspire to make the world a much better place to be in.

We line up under command of an American Major (Campbell) who is a fellow prisoner, and a German sergeant counts us. This is "Appel"—an institution we are to become more familiar with as time goes on. The German lt. col. who is commandant of the camp comes in, takes a salute and the report, and we file into the mess area.

And it's a good breakfast, something like those at the base. Coffee and toast and porridge, and afterwards we light cigarettes—still a great luxury to us—and consider the day's business.

We really have no duties at all—but we have things to do. Laundry, for instance. This is our first chance to clean up the filthy clothes we've been wearing.

No sooner said than done—on the laundry.

There is one ordinary galvanized tin bucket in the compound, and by dint of scouting and persuasion, we obtain it. We work by two's, "King" Cole shedding his dignity and his clothes (down to underwear shorts) to work with me.

This Cole is a perfect type of British officer—you can easily picture him in full dress and fitting it perfectly. Tall, lean, hawk-faced, grey at the temples, with a modulated voice an actor might envy. But, stripped to his underwear, with his bony knees near his head as he bends with rapt attention over a dirty sock, he is a far cry from a correct Britisher. No one sees anything ludicrous in it here.

My filthy white socks, dirty underwear, handkerchief (which has served me as a wash-rag, pillow-case, towel, etc.) go into the water and come out creditably clean.

And then, since this is real sunshine, and we feel the need of it, we haul our sacks out into the sun, strip, and soak up the heat. It's pleasant here in the sun. Our Englishmen, we find, have been familiar with the States—one took training there, the other visiting extensively, so they know our idiom and can discuss our meals and customs. They give us a good insight into their side of the war, their tactics and planes. They even attempt to explain the mysteries of cricket to us—with no great success.

By lunch-time, we're well cooked, so we retire inside. The Red Cross has provided cards, very much worn, but cards, and we get a bridge game going. And we begin to get the stories of some of the others here. The stories are curiously similar, though each is unique in some way—and they are all worth any writer's time. But this is not the place for them.

The Wrong Side of the Fence

A long, lazy day, and a blessed one to us, after the past weeks. We are acquiring the habit of living day-to-day, like animals. And so we are measurably happy with the present.

July 8, 1944
Wetzlar, Germany

Up again at "Appel", and the story goes the rounds that we leave here tonight for a permanent camp—Stalag Luft III. It will be a long train trip—three days, perhaps.

Meanwhile, it's another bright, clear day, and we have three more good meals to look forward to. The camp leader asks for volunteers to peel potatoes for lunch. Some of us sunned not wisely but too well yesterday, and we want to keep out of the sun now. And we feel the need to be doing something, so we volunteer.

We are probably the highest paid potato-peelers in the world at this writing. "King" Cole, whose rank corresponds to major; two American majors, three captains, and a bunch of second lieutenants including Cole, Post and myself.

The spuds are little and grubby and full of roots and frost-spots, and devilishly hard to peel and still have any potato left. But the talk is pleasant and the work progresses. A British sergeant, working in the kitchen, even makes us tea. It's hot and good.

After the evening meal, we are ordered to pack, and, each man carrying his own stuff, we move out of the compound, back to the building where we entered on arrival. Here we are searched again, sign a new parole for the trip, are warned that the guards have orders to shoot without warning at any attempt to escape, and are instructed in precise English by the camp commandant that the German people are "not kindly disposed toward" us. An American major (Campbell) is put in charge of us, and "King" Cole is in charge of food supplies. He asks Cole, Post, me, Lt. J. P. George (of whom more later) and two others to help him—we figure we can travel together that way.

And so we start back to the town. But it's a little different. We are clean, we have shoes, we are fed, our clothes are decent, our spirits are up. The walk, surprisingly, is even refreshing. Quite a difference from our walk the other way two days ago.

At the station we find two second-class carriages waiting for us. A real prison train, the cars have iron bars on the windows. One of them is of Italian make—it still carries ads for "Il Popolo De Italia—Fondatore Benito Mussolini" and other things Italian. It will be uncomfortable—they put eight men into each compartment, said compartments having been built for no more than six. But we are allowed to move about the car freely.

We eight who have volunteered, get a compartment, then go outside again to load on the food, which is to last us three days.

July, 1944

Bless the Red Cross again! This food is contained in small cardboard boxes—one box for each two men. And each box contains a can of coffee-extract, a can of dried milk, spam, corned beef, sardines, salmon, meat pate, cheese, raisins, a bar of chocolate.

This experience is making a good American out of me. Do I emphasize the food? Well, every bite I take reminds me that I was faring as well as the German troops a few days ago. And it was very poor fare indeed.

We got the food aboard, and are assured we'll get hot water later for coffee. We are better handled now—there's a German captain in charge of the shipment, and an official interpreter, so that we can communicate. It helps, to deal with another officer rather than with German enlisted men who seem to delight in pushing us around.

So, we're aboard, and nothing to do until an engine puts in an appearance. Next to our car is one of those funny little four-wheeled wagons they use for freight all over Europe, with a gang of nine Russians unloading it. They are husky fellows, and they stop their work every now and then to give us a big grin and the now familiar "V" signal. They seem completely unabashed by their heavily-armed guard. We grin back—that's about all we can do. Some of the Russ are wearing American flying clothes, we note.

Finally, at 10 P.M., we are hitched to a long freight train, and start to move out. Comes now the problem of fitting eight men in space too small for six. We shift about, and finally settle it when Post and George climb into the baggage racks, allowing the six remaining to dispose themselves foot-to-head across the seats. Not a very good arrangement since the seat backs are uncompromisingly straight and hard, and the space between is just big enough to make the body sag uncomfortably in the small of the back.

But we've been uncomfortably situated before.

July 9, 1944
En route

And it was a bad night. Everyone is cramped, stiff. Nobody got more than an hour or two of sleep. We seem to have spent a good part of the night sitting in sidings and freight yards, being cut into and out of freight trains.

There is a lot of railroad activity, however.

There's no water on the cars for washing—none at all, in fact, except a thermos-full for drinking. This brings another problem, too. The toilet in the car won't flush without water and the stench near it is getting bad.

But if we can't wash or shave, we can eat. And we do, lavishly. Even piggishly. But we're to be excused, I think. It's been long since we've had an abundance of food.

I'm telescoping this day because it was a long, weary one—a succession of railroad yard stops and slow runs between them. Again, the countryside is beautiful, so lushly green, so meticulously cared for. We pass through town after town where people come to stare at us.

The Wrong Side of the Fence

Finally, in the evening we pass through Dresden, and come to Leipzig. Here is evidence of good bombing—precision hits on buildings and factories, an airfield, and other targets.

And so for another bad night for sleeping—somehow more uncomfortable than last—we are more tired. Twelve days since we went down.

July 10, 1944
Sagan, Germany

This was a sorry-looking lot this morning. Sleepless again, bearded again, feeling dirty again after a miserable night. But we're healthy enough—everyone eating heartily. Our food packages have lasted amazingly well, eked out by German bread. We eight have nearly a full package left, and we'll be at Sagan at noon, we're told.

It's raining heavily, and continues to do so when we finally arrive at Sagan—a railroad yard east of the station and town, where we disembark.

After some formalities with the guards, we line up in the rain, looking forward to a long hike in the mud and wet. But it turns out to be only a couple of blocks, until we turn into a barbed-wire-studded gate, which slaps shut behind us, and we're in.

It's a German Truppenlager—troop camp—we're in. We go through it, through a second gate, and enter what we come to know as the Vorlager—main entrance to all prison compounds. A camp within a camp.

Here we go through another search, and then to a shower room, then to have our pictures taken again. The wounded are taken to a nearby barracks which serves as a hospital, and we march through still another gate.

And the minute we're through—we're back in our own army again, it seems.

In spite of the rain, there's a crowd of men around the gate, looking for friends among us.

It's good to see them, they're our kind. Clean cut and well set up, shaven, many in shorts, healthy—AMERICAN looking, I should say. They're a relief after the distinctly small, grubby German Army we've seen so far.

We're marched to a central building which turns out to be a very creditable theater—obviously home-made but as obviously American. And here is an American lt. col., directing things, with several captains and a major to help.

This, at last, is being done our way—by men whose authority we recognize, whose language we understand, whose methods we are used to.

These men are well organized, they are obviously prepared for our coming. Quickly, we are assigned to barracks, given brief instructions as to what we can expect immediately, and sent to a doctor—an American doctor—for a quick physical checkup. Post and I are to return tomorrow for further check ups on our troubles.

July, 1944

Do I emphasize "American"? I mean to. Never appreciated before how much that word meant.

And as to the barracks, where we are assigned to a combine (F) of twelve men with whom we will share our food and living quarters, and then to a cookhouse for a meal.

With splendid—and welcome—help from others in the combine, (Cole, Post and George being in the same group with me) we spend the remainder of the day getting spaces, filling sacks with wood-shavings for mattresses, getting settled. And the boys feed us at 6 P.M.

And then a formation—a real one—at 5 P.M. Taps—and how good it sounds! at 10 P.M. Lights out at midnight.

An eventful day, and a good one.

July 11, 1944
Sagan, Germany

Today we began to get organized as to our position here.

Last night we were given a brief address by the Senior American Officer, Col. D. T. Spivey. I remember his entrance as something of a shock—somehow it had never occurred to me that a man of his rank might be a prisoner. He is certainly "old Army", but we're glad of it. He seems fair and reasonable, and knows the value of discipline towards morale.

For example: The Germans require an "Appel" twice a day. We make them regular formations, forming as a parade in hollow square, under our own officers and our own commands. It helps a great deal, we are told, to maintain self-respect, and it gives a military point to our day. (More of that in another place.)

First, we find that this camp—Center Compound—is one of about five others in this immediate area, housing other American flyers, R.A.F. personnel, and some smaller camps of Poles, Czechs, French and Russians. Our compound is a sandy oblong, perhaps two and a half acres in area, cleared out of one of those carefully-tended pine forests we have seen all over Germany.

Eleven barracks, each now housing 130 men, and latrines cover about three quarters of the area. These barracks are long, low weather-beaten structures, providing shelter and nothing more. The remaining area is left open as a playing field, which ingenuity and patience have converted into a basketball court and two baseball diamonds and a soccer-football field.

The whole area is surrounded by a double barbed-wire fence, about 10 feet high, topped at each corner and along the East and West sides by high sentry-boxes, manned by heavily-armed guards.

Within the barbed-wire, some 25 yards inside it and all around the camp—is another fence. This is a light wooden paling only a foot or so in height. This is our dead-line, the "warning rail". A step inside it will bring an instant volley of shots from the guards, we are assured. Thus, this fence establishes a pretty thorough no-man's land between us and the main wire.

The Wrong Side of the Fence

In the barracks themselves, the accommodations are pretty crude. A room at either end contains a coal cooking stove, and another room a very elementary latrine. Floors are rough-hewn boards, as are the sidewalls and ceiling. Windows are equipped with heavy shutters for blackout purposes.

Within this building, 135 men are now housed. Their accommodations are simple. Double-deck beds such as we are now familiar with, with wood-shaving filled mattresses. No chairs, but a few benches, and one heavy table to each 12-man combine. This, plus cheap wooden lockers, constitutes the conveniences.

For other "conveniences", the Germans supply the aforementioned cooking stoves, a few lead "trinkvassers"—water pitchers—some china bowls and spoons, knives and forks. Period.

But American ingenuity is hard to beat.

With no tools except those of their own devising (since hammers, saws, and related tools are forbidden by the Germans because they might be used for escapes), with no materials except used tin cans and nothing else but patience, these men have succeeded in manufacturing all manner of very creditable cooking pots and pans, containers, bowls. They have built—again out of old tin cans—cracker grinders, coffee pots, ice-cream freezers, even a clock.

We who come in now have a great advantage. We can have all the benefits of the experience and ingenuity of those who have been here, some of them, for a year or more. (See Appendix #4.)

July 24, 1944
Sagan, Germany

Now that this narrative has covered the first few days, I'm going to stop carrying it as a day-to-day account. Things have too much of a sameness here, day to day, and paper is scarce.

Chapter 3

◆

August, 1944

August 1, 1944
Sagan

It seems impossible that I wrote the last brief entry six days ago, or that we've been in this camp for three weeks now. Or, even, that we've been a few days over a month since we arrived on German-held ground, June 29th.

I guess part of the reason the time goes so fast has its roots in our Army life previously. We are so used to having practically no privacy, to living with perfect strangers amicably because we must, to doing things in concert, to having little or nothing to say about our general future, that we fall into this way of life, too, with almost no reaction. And certainly, no friction.

Not to say that life is easy here. Lord knows, it is entirely possible for a man to do no more than the chores required of him by his combine, and spend the rest of his time doing absolutely nothing.

But for most of us, that's not the thing to do. Because if you have nothing to do, you start to think. And your thinking usually starts with reproach—either for yourself or others, your mind worrying at a thousand items. And then you get to thinking of home, and your wife, and the folks, and places you've been and things you've done and said. And then the barbed wire and the guards begin to get on your mind and nerves, and—but you can go mad that way, too. You can talk about these things, and think of them, too—but you must do it lightly, occasionally.

No, the trick is to keep yourself busy. Keep doing anything to have an object to be accomplished, even if that object is only the construction of a tin plate. There are other things too—this is the first chance many of us have had in years (me included) to do any serious reading, catch up on ourselves mentally. And, thanks to the Red Cross and the YMCA, we have a pretty fair library here, containing some 2000 volumes of all kinds. (See Appendix #5.)

Among the 1500 of us are men with considerable professional and educational backgrounds. Entirely on a voluntary basis, they have agreed to lay out and conduct courses in their own subjects. Result has been a regular school, offering some 27 courses in all, holding daily classes. It operates almost with-

The Wrong Side of the Fence

out textbooks, teachers supplying (by dictation) vocabularies, etc. Notebooks come in through the Red Cross at Geneva.

In addition to the school, there are other organized activities. These include a really excellent band, a choir, a theater group, two newspapers (one of which I have joined), a thorough sports program.

And the boys have built an excellent set of maps of the world, and on it they keep track of the progress of the war—as filtered to us through the medium of German news broadcasts. Additionally, there are discussion groups, Sunday church services.

To this, add the necessity of doing everything for yourself—since we have no laundries, cooks. We all wash our own socks and underwear and shirts and whatnot—all, including the Colonel. And washing includes heating water.

There's also the matter of taking baths. No such things here as taking a shower any time. One day a week we can take the briefest of showers—but we must take them at the Germans' convenience, not ours.

So most of us heat up water on the stove, and take supplementary baths out of tin pails. Something, anyway.

Sounds like a pretty busy schedule, doesn't it? But, remember, it's all "made" work. You have to keep pushing yourself to do it—for there's really no object to it; it doesn't get you out of here any faster. Even sports can pall.

Because there's always the wire around you. Always the towers with the guards and the machine guns in them. Always no place to go, no relief to be had. No prospect of a beer-bust at the end of the week, or a date in town, or just something new in the way of scenery to look at. No more of the feeling of freedom—of owning the earth—that flying gives you (even though you curse it, even though you say you hate it).

So you push yourself, become involved in a hundred small affairs until you are convinced you really are doing something worthwhile. And you are, of course.

Amazingly, in such a place, you broaden your horizons. Because we are living now much closer to each other than we ever have before, because there is no such thing as getting away from each other, we find we must make more concessions to each other, must make an effort to get the other man's point of view and understand it. And we have time, for once, to give some thought to that point of view, and understand it.

And we have time for something else too. Time to consider the future. Not our own, directly—on that we tread lightly—but the world and the war. We've seen something of war, all of us, and that world of the future will be our world. Our discussions are serious and sound. For a lot of us who are quite young, and for many more of us who are not accustomed to thinking this way—it's an excellent thing. Maybe, if we have sense enough to voice some of the things we've thought about when we get home, we can do something about straightening things out. Some of our thoughts are pretty large—but it's a large problem we consider.

A good thing.

August 2, 1944
Sagan

Following this up today, since the weather is miserable and rainy and several projects (such as clothes washing) have had to be postponed. So, back to my account of how we live.

Basic unit of our lives here is the combine—an organization of from four to twelve men, put together arbitrarily as always in the Army. In this group we live, find our friends, have our prison being.

Our combine, for example, contains 12 men. It is assigned an area within the barracks of about 20 x 15 feet. In this space we have six double beds, six lockers, a big table, two long benches, a couple of stools, a double-locker in which we keep food supplies, a bench along the side (where we have no windows), holding our few cooking utensils.

It is a small, crowded space—would be for two men, let alone 12. It takes real cooperation to live so close to others without friction. A man has no place to go to be alone. If he's in a bad mood or easily annoyed, it's no place for him.

We do our own cooking. We are fed by a combination of German-issued rations—which include mostly black bread and grubby potatoes, with an occasional head of cabbage or some kohlrabi; and the Red Cross container given each man each week. This container—with its meats, butter, tinned vegetables, etc., is our staple.

Originally, all this food was lumped and cooked together for a whole camp. But in the interest of variety—and for something to do—we now do our own cooking. Each man in the combine takes his turn as cook, cooking three meals a day for a week at a time. To assist him, the remaining men serve one day, in turn, as KP—being responsible for washing dishes, pots and pans, keeping the combine area clean by sweeping and mopping and assisting the cook. A real job, too.

None of us, of course, are cooks—few ever touched a skillet. But as usual, it's amazing what a man can do if he must. Some have developed into very competent cooks and can do wonders with as dainty as cake or tasty a stew as ever their mothers did. Recipes are exchanged with the same avidity here as at any sewing circle at home.

We have no flour. But we have heavy biscuits—and out of our tin-can cracker grinders we can produce excellent flour. We've made some pretty weird combinations—like canned salmon, canned bacon, cracker-flour and onions—into very tasty dishes.

There are practically no fresh vegetables available, but we have our own. Under Col. Spivey's orders, every available inch of the poor, sandy soil has been cultivated. And, using the crudest of hand-made tools, we've managed to raise respectable crops of radishes, carrots, kale, lettuce, onions and whatnot.

Which both provides healthful food, and something to do.

This is an incongruous place to stick this in, but I want to note it down.

The Wrong Side of the Fence

We had an accession of rank last week, with the arrival of Brig. Gen. A. W. Vanaman. We now have a general, five full colonels, and seven lieutenant colonels as fellow-prisoners.

August 7, 1944
Sagan

Wrote to Ann day before yesterday, but it's so very hard to write to anyone from here. There is so little I am permitted to say.

Been thinking over the situation here and have come to the conclusion that the worst part of this business is the uncertainty—that and the fact that there's absolutely nothing that we here can do towards bringing the thing to an end.

Always, before, there was a definite date ahead. Something to count on or look forward to. In a year you would get your commission. In a month you'd be an upper classman. In two weeks you'd move to another post. If you finished 30 missions (under criteria in effect in 1943), you could go home.

But here, where we have nothing to do but mark the time going by, we have no dates, no objective. We avidly watch the crawl of the allied forces across the maps—progress given us by German news broadcasts, and we make guesses, bets on the end of it.

But we don't know. And we can't do anything to help.

This life wouldn't be too bad, if you knew it was going to last for a month more—even two, three months. But not to know at all is maddening. And some of these boys have been here a year already. And some of the British over the fence there, have been here five years.

Don't take it from this that I'm discouraged. I'm not—I don't think it can possibly last more than a short time more. But I don't know.

And, getting away from that subject, I've taken up a new activity—fencing. Haven't done any since I left high school, but find a couple of boys here who can do it. The camp has a couple of foils.

August 10, 1944
Sagan

Another three days have gone by, and I haven't written letters to anyone. I should, but I keep giving myself the excuse that there isn't anything to write, and it'll take too long, and such. All true, but I should write anyway. As in some other things, I find myself adopting a "manana" attitude. I have so much time, and really nothing to do but fool it away.

Hence the note today. I do have some work—some pieces I promised to write for the week's issue of the camp paper. But I don't feel like doing the work. So I figure rambling on like this might help.

This is an odd life we lead in many ways.

For instance, we have no money at all. True, under the Geneva Convention, we are paid in Reichsmarks, the equivalent of what a German officer of our rank receives—some $28 per month in my case.

August, 1944

But there's nothing that we could use the money for really, so by agreement some time ago, the money is held in a camp pool for use in mass purchase of anything available. There are several million marks now, there being nothing to purchase.

Still, within the compound we find a need for some system of exchange—some way to obtain things others may have, for a fair value. For example, the older men who have been here some time, have received packages from home, which may contain more cigarettes than they need. But they, in turn, may need a pocket comb that one of us has.

So an organization we know as "Foodaco" has been set up to operate as a store, its prices based on an elaborate point system. For example, a pack of American cigarettes is worth 10 points, a bar of candy 50 points. And if you like tea, you can swap your coffee ration for tea at a set price.

It works out pretty well, all told.

This week, to keep things going, we emptied out a big brick static water tank (about 40 x 40) that stands in the middle of the compound for emergency use; cleaned it out and refilled it to make a "swimming pool". But the water is awfully cold—I'll wait a day or so before I go in. We swim naked—no suits, and it's cleaner that way.

Also, we're to have a movie—the third shown here in more than a year, they tell me. "Dixie Dugan"—an oldie, but we'll all go, of course.

There were some German POW's—repatriates from the U.S.—here last week. They told of getting into towns, movies, ice cream, etc. It hurts a little.

We seem so far from that.

And, of course, we must depend on ourselves for most of our entertainment. So there's to be a play next week—"The Front Page". To run for seven nights.

Hope it is good. Will be. Real talent here.

August 10, 1944
Sagan

Let this ride for a while. Realize I'm getting myself into a bad mood. But on talking to others who have been here longer, find it to be quite a common state of nerves.

We live on hopes—and we live only for the future. What we do from day to day is only incidental to that great day when we are free.

So, when the news we get is good—when advances are made—we feel good, spirits are high, things seem worthwhile. Contrarily, when things newswise are static (as at present) we don't feel so gay, we are serious, we extend our long thoughts to even longer vistas of time. And we really do live very close together—and bad weather and lack of anything with an object to do makes us harder to get along with, and we must be very careful because there's no place for real trouble.

The Wrong Side of the Fence

We call ourselves "Kriegie" (from Kriegsgefangener—war prisoners) and this trouble we call "Kriegie-itis".

There's only one thing to hang onto. A thing I know from past experience. It is that time does march on.

In a year from now I'll be reading these notes as something that happened in the far past. But it's hard to keep that in mind when you have to just sit and let it pass.

So, I must cling to it—time WILL pass, and this will be a phase in my life and no more. And now, having unburdened myself thus on paper—I better go to work.

August 13, 1944
Sagan

This is Sunday, and I've been on the ground now just two days over six weeks; in the camp a little over four weeks.

Not very long, really, but sometimes—as in other places in the Army before this—I catch myself feeling as if I'd always been here, as if the other existence I remember had never been, but was only one of those half-remembered things you see in dreams.

The monotonous regularity of the days make for this apparently long vista of time behind me.

However, by the same token the very monotony of the days makes the time pass more quickly in the end. Just don't notice time slipping by.

Well, let 'er slip, say I! Sooner the better.

And to continue with how we live:

Standard costume is shirt and shorts, or just shorts. The shorts are homemade, but entirely practical. It's summer and plenty warm, for one thing. For another, most of us have only one pair of pants—which would soon wear out in constant use. And you don't wear underwear shorts under the shorts—so you save laundry.

Before the present camp command took over a year ago, I understand, there was considerable laxity about what the men wore—many wearing nothing at all whenever possible. But now we wear shirts to all formations, and on Saturdays appear in as near full dress uniform as we can scrape together. From a morale standpoint, it's a good thing.

And as always in the Army, we have our own slang. Here, we don't "gripe", we "bleed". When something goes wrong, we say we've "had it". And we've borrowed the British "Good Show" to express approval of anything.

Later, August 13

Left this for a while to go out and watch a baseball and then a soccer game. Lt. Col. Purinton, who acts as recreation director here, has done well. There is always something like that going on. Gets us out in the air.

August, 1944

There's a German airfield somewhere north of us—a sort of transition school, we gather. Anyway, a bunch of FW-190's maneuver around pretty often, practicing formation flying. Every now and then, one of them gives us a buzz job. That's a sweet airplane, and those boys can fly. It's a refined form of torture, though—we'd give a lot to be flying up there.

The movies we were promised last week didn't materialize—projector broke down, and of course no replacements are available. So the play will be our sole entertainment.

Yesterday we had a long evening recording program—the boys have built a P.A. system for this purpose—records from "Oklahoma", "The Chocolate Soldier" and others.

Very pleasant, but made me homesick.

August 16, 1944
Sagan

We've been expecting a new purge of men from the interrogation centers for several days now—a purge being a group of men cleaned out of the Dulag after questioning. The Germans usually wait until they have captured 50 or more men, then send them on here in a bunch.

We wait with mixed emotions. They'll bring news from home direct—maybe of our friends at the base. And Dave might be among them. Cole, Post and I would give a lot to see that boy again.

But a new purge will make trouble too. We house 135 men in these barracks now, and they shouldn't house more than 70, and with the new purge we will be forced up to 142 men. It will be terribly overcrowded—worse as winter draws near and we are forced to spend more time indoors. But it begins to look as if we may not have to worry about the winter months here. News is looking good.

Amazing, the effect of news on our morale. Of course, we've nothing to do but watch it avidly. We are impatient with it. A 30-mile Allied advance is big, we know, but all we can see is how very small it is in comparison to the distance that must be covered before we go home.

Last week, for about three days, we had little or no news. The weather was hot and lazy, and morale went down and down—mine included, as evidenced by what I wrote.

And then, three days ago, the Germans announced Allied landings in South France. You could actually see the morale start zooming up like the mercury in a thermometer. And all week now, the news has shown a steady progress—and our spirits stay up.

We are over-optimistic. But we have become pretty good judges and armchair strategists. We all have some knowledge of things military and, because we can read the German propaganda from the inside (we get German newspapers too) we have a pretty fair idea of how things are going outside.

The Wrong Side of the Fence

We are lavish, thus, with our predictions, and under the spell of good news we are willing to bet our most valued possession—chocolate bars—on our predictions.

The play "The Front Page" is on this week—saw it last night and am amazed again at what these boys can do with almost nothing but ingenuity and a sense of humor. The setting was perfect. And it passed the evening.

Going to Spanish class this morning, I overheard our general teaching German to the five colonels. He (the General) speaks it fluently, they don't. It was amusing.

But official dignity is official dignity, so I only caught a glimpse (and a few words) and left.

August 22, 1944
Sagan

Another six days have passed, and things progress, news-wise, notably in France. Good show.

The new purge arrived last night, and Dave was not among them. We got 100 men for this compound (center compound)—the rest went to other camps. Anyway, it makes the place more crowded.

Continuing with life here:

Our favorite card games are bridge, hearts and cribbage (and solitaire) in that order. At most Army posts, poker takes precedence. But it's axiomatic that you must have something to bet before you can play the game. And we have no money.

Once in a while, the boys do get up a poker game, using an elaborate system of point values for betting—but the things we have to bet are too valuable to us for much of this. After all, you can always borrow a few dollars if you're broke. But it's very difficult to borrow cigarettes or chocolate.

Most of our betting is confined to ball games and the end of the war.

We have some of the most gorgeous sunsets here that I have ever seen, and some of the best cloud formations. Although the last few days were clear, always in the evening huge clouds grow up on our horizon and some sailing majestically across the blue sky, tinted in all the colors from white to deep rose-red.

I think my memory of Sagan will always picture the camp enclosed in a square of green pines, with the foliage only on the top, and a bright sky filled with great, brightly-white billowy clouds.

That, and the sound of railroad trains near at hand. There's a railroad yard just outside of camp, and the sound of whistles and escaping steam is never far off. Although I seem to have noted a recent lessening of activity there.

The days are becoming appreciably shorter, though—dusky by 9 P.M., dark at 10. The summer is ending, with that sadness in the air that Fall always brings for me.

August, 1944

Got a haircut the other day. No barbers, of course, but in their time here some of the boys have become pretty handy with the scissors. As with everything else, got to make things—and talent—do.

As summer ends, the flies get worse. We have no screens, and the Germans won't let us make any, because they would cut off a clear view from outside.

But 142 men living and sleeping and eating in one place will attract flies. To make it worse, the cans in which most of our food comes are punched full of holes (to insure that they are not kept for use in escapes) and in this hot weather they too attract the flies. It's getting to the point where we don't stay indoors during the day—the flies become too annoying. We can only try for as much sanitation as we can achieve, to combat the trouble.

By the way, the movies finally came in. I see the show tonight.

August 24, 1944
Sagan

My birthday—I'm now 28. The news is sort of a present (Allies doing well in France). And the combine made a cake to mark the occasion.

Fourth of July in a cell, birthday in prison.

But there seems to be good prospect that this Christmas and New Year's and Ann's Birthday (Jan. 2), may be celebrated at home and in an appropriate manner. So I guess I can stand this. Though a birthday or any such occasion here—for a guy as introspective as myself—is odd. Turns thoughts to home and other scenes.

My celebration consisted of my first running since I've been here—the perimeter of the compound is a bit over 1000 yards, and I found to my great surprise that I could make it all around at a fair dog-trot without falling over on my face and gasping like a fish.

I shall continue to run. Want to keep in shape.

I've been much interested to watch the workings of the propaganda machine, as reflected by the news we get, and the newspapers.

Best device I've noted is the telling of the news more or less in full, with a long string of towns and places named, but no explanation of the significance attached.

Without a map handy, therefore, the accounts are almost meaningless to the general public, I imagine. Just as meaningless as if you told an average American that there was fighting in Peapack, N.J. It's only in connection with Peapack's nearness to New York that the information is of value to the casual listener.

So it is possible to report the news in this manner (and saying only that there is action near this town or that) without having it sound too bad.

In the meantime, as the lines continue to creep toward us, the camp morale remains high.

The Wrong Side of the Fence

August 26, 1944
Sagan

Saturday—and with it the weekly standby inspection. Surprising what a good-looking crowd we are when dressed in our carefully-preserved remnants of uniforms, shaved, shined and slicked up. Believe it's good for our morale to see each other thus dressed once in a while.

And a band concert, as usual, this afternoon will pass the time.

As we visibly approach the time when we'll be going home again (since the news looks so good) our thoughts turn more and more to what we'll do in those happy days when we shall attain our status as civilians.

Our endless arguments and discussions, of course, must omit the fact that we really don't know what the Army plans to do with us when we return to its control. Aside from that, the discussions are certainly interesting.

I and those others (like Cole) who, by accident of age or circumstances have professions or experience in business to return to, are very fortunate—even though changes have undoubtedly been made in our fields.

But we are the minority here. Most of these men are too young to have established themselves. Of 1597 men in the compound at this writing, the average age is 22 years. And it will be very hard for a lot of these men to go back to school. To step at once from the status of an officer to that of a student will be difficult. I know it was hard enough for me, when I entered cadets.

There's another thing too—economics. Some of these lads of 19 and 20 have been earning $300 a month or more—a stupendous salary for a man that age. Certainly far more than most can hope to command for many years in civilian life under anything approaching normal circumstances.

Many will try to remain in the Army, but it's hard to conceive of a peacetime Air Force large enough to accommodate all the men who may want to remain in it. A mitigating circumstance is our imprisonment, which has shown us a clearer set of standards of contentment and requirements for living happily.

A serious problem, and we give much thought to it. To help, some of the men with practical experience have formed a discussion panel to outline business methods, outlines and requirements. Good idea.

August 28, 1944
Sagan

Should have noted that the long-awaited movie finally was shown—"Dixie Dugan". And this week we have another, even older, "The Corsican Brothers". I saw it with Ann a couple of years ago. But it's indubitably entertainment—and I shan't miss it. Two movies in two weeks! Such prosperity is amazing.

Statistics: We have now 1597 men in this compound, crowded into the eleven barracks. The roster of rank includes one brigadier general, six full colonels, four lieutenant colonels, 11 majors, 47 captains, 64 flight officers, 116 non-coms, and the rest second and first lieutenants.

August, 1944

Germans have announced they intend to send another 300 men in here—so we may yet see Dave—but this will force the use of tents in addition to the barracks. Things are really going to be crowded.

The news of the war continues good from our viewpoint, Paris being mostly in our hands and Rumania having capitulated, according to the German broadcasts. However, as after the invasion of Southern France, our excitement has calmed down a bit. We are still very optimistic, and spirits good.

But we've settled down to the idea that it will be a couple of months yet before we're free. My own private prediction is Nov. 1.

Germans here, like the poor, are always with us. But we studiously pay no attention to them, and they say little or nothing to us.

In addition to the "Postens" who man the six sentry-boxes 24 hours a day, there are a number of men whom we call "ferrets" who are in the compound all the time. They just walk around keeping an eye on things in general, looking in at the windows, walking unannounced through the barracks. And there are extra armed guards when we have formations and suchlike. To top it, when we are locked into the barracks every night at dark, the "Hundsfuehrer"—guards with dogs—come into the compound with their dogs, and spend the night patrolling.

When any orders are given, however, they are passed to us by our own officers, not often directly by the Germans. When, occasionally, we must speak to them, we address them as "Mister", with no attention to rank. They respond in kind.

Most of these guards are older men, and they give the impression that they'd rather be home than here—but rather here than at the front.

Group of "Ferrets" of German Army, assigned to wander around camp, see and hear what they could. No names available.

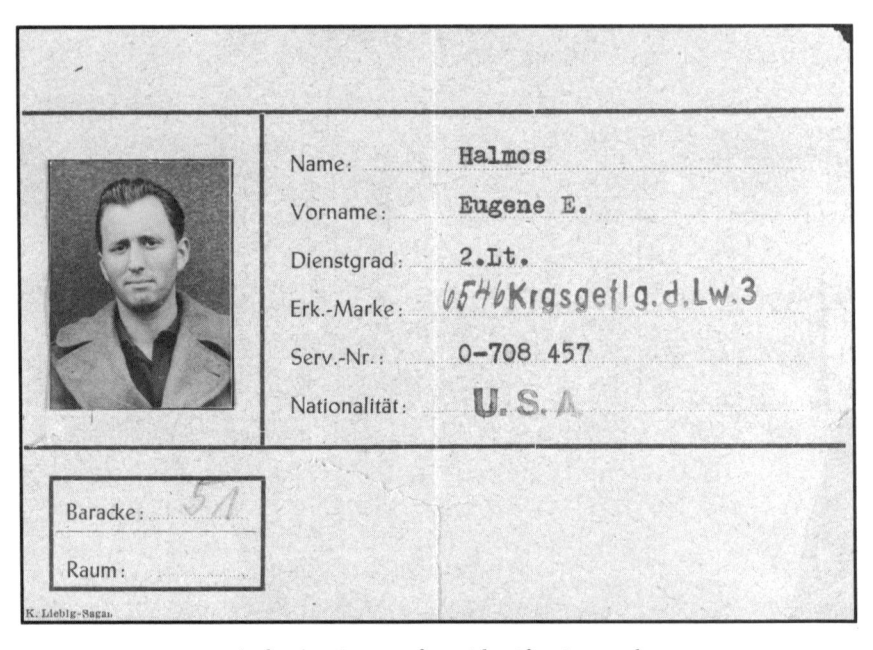

Name:	**Halmos**
Vorname:	**Eugene E.**
Dienstgrad:	**2.Lt.**
Erk.-Marke:	6546 **Krgsgeflg.d.Lw.3**
Serv.-Nr.:	**0-708 457**
Nationalität:	**U.S.A**

Baracke: 51
Raum:

Author's prisoner of war identification card.

Overall view of camp at Moosburg. Despite weather, many of more than 100,000 prisoners assembled here had to be housed in tents shown, since there was no room for any more in existing barracks. Rumor was that Hitler planned to surround his "castle" at Berchtesgarten with prisoners, on theory that Allies would not fight through their own men, hence he could bargain for a deal. This was never done, however.

Scenes on march from Sagan that ended at Moosburg (see diary). Snow, ice on roads, German guards marching along (not shown, other guards with dogs on other side). Men tried to take along what they could in way of supplies and clothes— some on makeshift sleds.

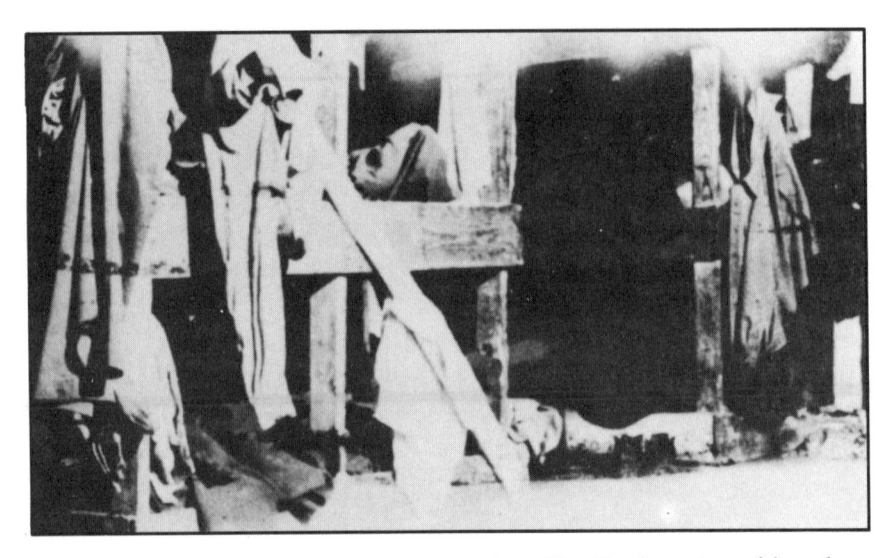

Sleeping arrangements, both at Sagan and Moosburg. Wood bunks, in tiers of three deep, no closets or storage areas, so all possessions had to be hung or placed around one's sleeping area; "mattresses" of sacks filled with sawdust and wood shavings, very narrow clearance between bunks.

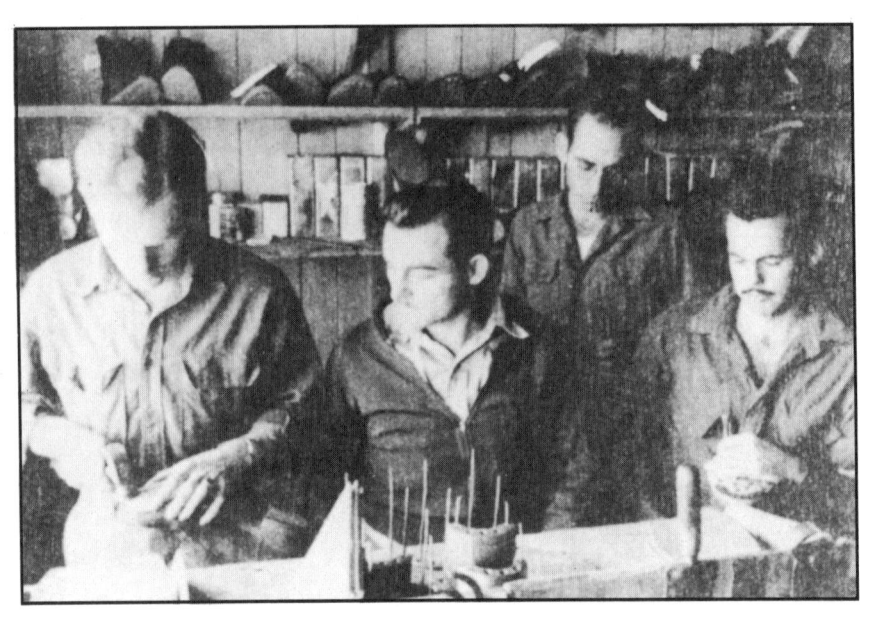

"Carpenter" shop in operation. Principal materials, flattened tin cans, old table knives (which served as hammers, cutting tools, etc.). Prisoners also tried to repair shoes, and other leather goods (on shelf behind man), as best possible.

*One result of "carpentry"—vent pipe made of attached cans
that originally contained powdered milk (KLIM), and powdered coffee.*

Close-up views of fences and guard towers, all of wood.

A couple of prisoners "walking the perimeter", only place where man could be alone. Note low fence —this was "deadline"—marking off a space about 20 ft. wide between campground and fence, where nobody dared step without permission of guards in towers.

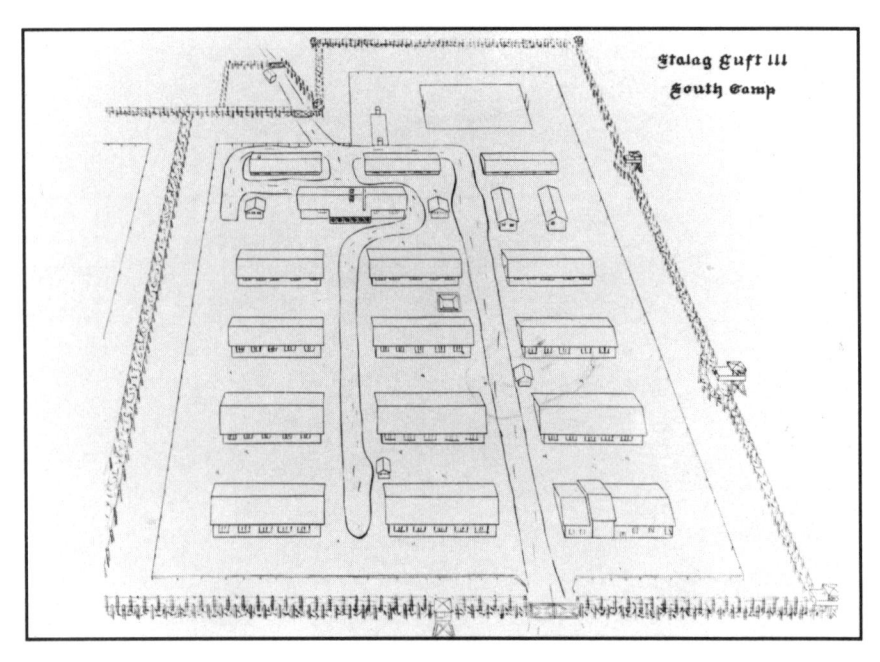

Sketch of camp layout. This was "south compound"—we were in "center compound" just adjacent to this, but layout was same. In our case, "playing field" shown as outlined spot at center, top here, was in center of barracks. Area shown as fenced at top left was "vorlager" where camp (German) officials held office space. "Deadline" is shown by light barbed wire line inside outer fence.

Interior views of camps, showing central "parade" ground, with barracks in rear (where prisoners assembled daily (very early in A.M.) for "Appel"—roll call. Prisoners made this a military formation, with men assembling as "companies" (by barracks) for sake of morale. Note the ever-present guard towers and fence.

Our "library"—end of one of the barracks, where books supplied by Red Cross stocked prisoner-built shelves. Only warm place in barracks; only place reasonably well lighted in long periods of darkness.

Confusing to new arrivals, apparent "women" in camp. These were prisoners who appeared in numerous plays, staged by camp personnel. Some of them, as shown here, made creditable appearance as women.

*Classes in "Sagan University"—conducted by prisoners who had
had real educational advantages.
"Credits" issued here were later accepted by many U.S. colleges and universities.*

Moosburg. When first U.S. tank of rescuing force (Patton's Third Army) crashed through barbed wire and entered camp, it was immediately covered by exultant P.O.W.s to the point where the tank (Sherman) was no longer visible.

Chapter 4

◆

September, 1944

September 1, 1944
Sagan

Never have I lived so intimately with flying bugs—flies, bees, moths, and other such insects. As mentioned before, we can't have screens, and the food attracts them. You go to bed with them buzzing in your ears, and you wake up in the morning with them dive-bombing your head.

The flies are the worst. There's a bees-nest someplace under the barracks near our windows—but the bees mostly mind their own business. They come in, settle on the jam or sugar, fill up and take off.

There's a sort of armed truce between us and the bees. They don't take much and they're clean, so we don't bother them—or they us—unless we get into competition for the same bit of sweets. In resulting tussles, some have been stung.

But the flies are an unmitigated nuisance. We're all glad the weather is turning cooler—it'll keep them down.

I've settled down now to shaving three times a week—Monday, Wednesday and Friday—as the best compromise between looking and feeling clean and the shortage of razor blades.

Everybody who gets here seems to get the whisker fever, and luxuriant mustaches, side-burns and other hirsute adornments grown are awful to behold. Then, one by one, the beards disappear and their owners emerge a little shamefacedly from behind them and settle down to shaving regularly and completely.

The same thing applies to the shaving of the head. Of course the business of getting a haircut is difficult, and it's hard to keep your hair clean with all this sand continually blowing and our lack of bathing facilities.

So every now and again a man will appear with a completely nude dome, gleaming whitely over a browned face. His example will be followed by a few more, until general ribbing brings the fad to a halt.

Lately, though, what with some prospect of a near end to this business, the fad has faded. No one wants to go home looking like that.

The Wrong Side of the Fence

Tense scene: On the baseball field the other day. Teams representing our barracks and the camp staff are playing. Col. Spivey, on third, is knocked down by a runner. Everybody leaves his post, runs to make sure he's OK. Game proceeds after Col. gets up.

Tom Mulligan, who runs the "Kriegie Times" has quit publication. So I've transferred my loyalties to Ron Delaney, who runs the "Gefangenen Gazette". Got to keep myself busy one way or another.

Statistics: Our "Kriegie Kollege" now offers some 25 courses—in languages, law, engineering, math, drawing, philosophy and whatnot, employs some 20 instructors, has a total attendance of more than a third of the camp's complement.

News is still good—Germans announce loss of Verdun and Amiens today.

September 5, 1944
Sagan

Yesterday was Labor Day, fifth year of the war (we are very history-minded) and for us was marked by four events, most important of which I'll list here, since I must elaborate on it.

First, we had an all-day sports program, starting with a parade of our band, then a track meet, baseball, basketball and soccer games. To inspire rivalry, we divided the camp into "East" and "West"—using the Mississippi River as a line of demarcation—and picked best players in each sport. Result was some remarkable games, the "East" sweeping three events, but losing baseball rather badly.

Second, a new purge arrived—some 100 men, bringing our population to over 1700 men.

Dave, again, wasn't among them, though Post, Cole and I scrutinized them all.

But a new purge always brings new faces and new stories, so we're glad to have them. These fellows are unfortunate in that they must live in the tents recently erected in the compound.

Third event was the knowledge of the war's fifth year, coupled with the news that the Allies are in Alsace and Belgium, according to the OKW [Oberkommando der Wehrmacht].

And fourth, there was the somewhat grim announcement that, starting next Monday, we must go on half rations of Red Cross food. This is of course a most serious matter.

Transportation, or rather lack of it, between here and Geneva, and Geneva and neutral ports, is the reason. At the moment, we understand that in camp there is an accumulation of stores for about three months of full rations. But with the increasing strength of the camp personnel, and the uncertainty of the duration of the war, it seems a prudent move to limit ourselves now against the possibility of real shortages later.

We all hope we'll be out of here soon, but we'd be fools not to attempt to provide for any possibility we can foresee.

September, 1944

So. This combine, for example, is now allotted 12 food parcels each week. Each parcel contains, roughly, seven pounds of food (not a whole lot for an entire week); in these, items include a can of powdered milk, a can of butter, a can of jam, a can of soluble coffee, two cans of meats, a bar of chocolate (or cocoa), five packs of cigarettes, a half-pound of sugar, a can of meat pate, a bar of soap, a bar of cheese, package of dried raisins or prunes, a can of salmon, two cans of sardines, a box of K-2 biscuit.

We have been accustomed to pooling these things in a general pot (except the candy which is precious to us), and from it make meals for all, supplemented a very little by the German-issued rations of a small amount of potatoes, black bread, and occasionally cooked barley.

Our problem now will be to cook less food, make it go further. We're going to be pretty fair food economists when we get home, if nothing else.

September 7, 1944
Sagan

The battle progresses apace, both on the East and West. Rumania has fallen, Finland has fallen, all France is in our hands, as well as half of Belgium and some of Holland.

And the betting here now runs that we'll be released within four weeks. I have never hoped for anything more fervently in all my life than that it be so. It seems to me I'd settle for anything, just to get out of here and back home.

Though most of our thoughts and all of our hopes are centered on the end of the war, yet none of us can quite visualize the occurrence itself. Somehow, I can't quite picture the announcement that will say that the war is over, that I am free.

One thing that is endlessly interesting to us is our own stories. They seem to bear endless repetition, and seem to be ever-interesting even to the others.

Of course, individually the event that brought us here was probably the most exciting of our lives. But that it should be fascinating to the others is a surprise. Because they all start the same way—the early briefing at some base in Italy or England, the flight to the target, the jump in the 'chute or the crash-landing, the capture, the interrogation, the arrival here.

But it is in the sameness of the beginning and the endless variation that brought the end that the fascination lies. As a newspaperman once, the stories that are living here drive me wild with my own inability to write them, to hear them all, even. I am not even certain that I could in any way do them justice.

For there are tremendous tales of great heroism—and great cowardice too— here. Men who live next to you, play games with you and argue with you are heroes beyond compare.

One of the mildest fellows you meet on the perimeter track sat grimly at the controls of a burning, bullet-riddled plane, holding it steady more by willpower than the scrap of control-surfaces, until his crew was out and he could save himself. This man stood to his guns to the last to cover his buddies; that man was horribly burned trying to stave off disaster; the one over here lost a finger in the knife-cold of high altitude, trying to help another.

The stories are endless, more daring than most fiction writers would dare to use as plots. And I am not the man to do them justice. Maybe no-one can, but it should be tried. These men are worthy of their heritage.

September 8, 1944
Sagan

A thought I've been cooking over—in re being here—is that we here, once at least, have stepped beyond mediocrity.

If we never do much else in our lives, we can cling to that one thing. We have answered a question in the affirmative that I think every man must ask himself.

For we have faced the supreme test—we have looked at death—and found we were not wanting. We found that, perhaps even without conscious thought, we had the courage and the will to do what we must do. And we have lived to know we did it.

That, if nothing else, should mark us as men apart—we and the others who have done as much in this war.

September 11, 1944
Sagan

Spirits a bit low right now—combination of the weather, slow news and short rations. Weather has been cold—damp cold, that goes right through you—and we have no means of heating the barracks as yet. Result being a depression which doesn't get much lift from the fact that we are on half-rations and always hungry.

And the news is slow for us—Germans only admitting Allied gains that look terribly small on our maps. It's fairly obvious that both sides are getting lined up for the final battle, and we know that the decision (in our favor of course) cannot be long delayed once that battle is joined. But it's just that old business of waiting—not knowing anything definite.

It's getting very hard for us to consider the war any longer from an even partially disinterested standpoint. To us, every move brings help nearer or takes it farther away. Every move seems to be aimed at getting us out of here. Indeed, sometimes it seems to us that the Allied strategy can have no other purpose.

Heard an excellent definition of a Kriegie argument—one of the interminable, pointless, often acrimonious discussions we're always getting into:

"A positive statement on a general subject; followed by a categorical denial; followed by mutual recriminations; followed by angry silence."

Statistics: Our reference library contains some 1200 volumes. Most heavily read being books on Math, Business, History, in that order.

September, 1944

September 13, 1944
Sagan

Another air-raid alarm yesterday, and this time we saw them through our windows. As usual, we are forced to go into the barracks by the Germans (we have no air-raid shelters) during the raid.

But through the windows we saw them—four flights of B-17's, high up and to the south of us, glinting silver in the sun. Did our hearts good to see them, though we were envious too. Those men up there were heading home—and we could only stand and watch them go.

And almost immediately after the raid, we had a search. Germans make us get out of the barracks, lock the doors, and then dug the place apart pretty thoroughly, looking for escape preparations, radios, etc., ripping up floorboards, checking through the lockers, looking for "contraband". Made it a very long morning for us.

◆ ◆ ◆

I've a kitten asleep on my bed as I write this.

One of Timoshenka's latest batch. Timoshenka is the compound's cat, and she seems imbued with the idea that it is her bounden duty to populate this entire section of Germany with kittens.

Anyway, she's forever having them. And we keep them (such as aren't killed by the dogs) because they are little and cute—and we need something like pets to lavish affection on.

Weather gets colder and more uncomfortable. Makes it harder to get up in the morning, keep warm during the night.

September 16, 1944
Sagan

Things on the front seem to be moving ponderously, grinding towards a finish to this business. But to us, as ever, it seems to be moving so very slowly.

We are sensible, of course, to the perils and hardships being faced by those men who are driving toward us, while we are comparatively comfortable and safe here, with nothing to do but think of ways to keep ourselves busy.

But we are not ashamed and not humble over being here. Most of us have added our weight—some, as myself, only a very little weight—to the victory that is so surely coming.

And the fact that we're here, instead of dead, wounded, or still at it, is the fortunes of war, and nothing else.

In a move designed (so the order reads) To improve discipline and efficiency, we have started to march to morning Appel, in regular formation. We line up before our barracks now each morning, and march in formation to the athletic field. (See Appendix #6.)

It's a surprise to us that the Germans permit it—they have always been afraid of allowing us any really military organization for fear of a mass break

The Wrong Side of the Fence

or action—but it does improve the situation considerably, making it easier for them to count us.

And anyway, we interpret it as an additional sign that we're going home soon, getting us used to a little more discipline against the day when we're back to our own again.

Food situation is not good. Not that we're starving, but we're always hungry—never seem able to be satisfied after a meal, somehow.

This isn't good at all—particularly since we have a shortage of coal (transportation again) which makes it possible for us to have only one hot meal a day. So we confine ourselves to one slice of black bread and coffee for breakfast (hot water being obtained from our kitchen); two slices of bread and tea for lunch, and a hot meal—but only a plateful per man—for supper. Not much for a gang of healthy, grown men.

Our command has taken some steps to alleviate the situation. Our kitchen—which up to now has been providing only hot water, has discovered a store of pea-soup powder (horrible, bilious-green stuff) and will put out hot soup for us three days each week. We can thicken and make the soup palatable by adding potatoes.

And the Germans have, at least temporarily, added to their ration to us. Incidentally, in the matter of German-issued rations, they are very far away from the Geneva Convention. Under it, we should receive the same food allowance as a German officer of our rank—and we couldn't live that well by far on the six slices of black bread, six or seven potatoes, and little barley that they actually give us.

But now they've brought in more potatoes, and just lately kohlrabi—great purple things full of stringy meal, but edible. And "blutwurst" which is a far cry from the blood sausage we knew at home. This stuff looks as if it was made after the complete slaughtering process was finished, and they stuffed in everything they had left. It's full of veins or gristle and bones. But it is food (it says here) and we must accept it as such.

Main question is how to cook the stuff so we can eat it. And like everything else here, small as it may seem at a distance, it's a problem of major importance to us.

September 17, 1944
Sagan

Meant to write more yesterday, but was interrupted, first by Appel, then supper, and then helping Delaney with the paper. And that, plus a peripatetic bridge game, rounded out my day pretty well.

Haven't written any letters at all this month. Can't get away from the idea that we'll be out of here and on our way home far ahead of any mail that I could send now.

And I haven't heard from home now in so very long—my last letter (in England) was dated June 10—that I have no idea what goes on there—whether Ann is back in New York or still in the mid-west, or anything. But, I fervently

September, 1944

hope, another couple of weeks will see me in a position to find out these things and many more.

For me, though, the suspense is building up and up. The Allies are in Aachen now, inside Germany, that is. Remains to be seen how long the Germans will hold on.

I think I ought to mention it again that this forced incarceration and idleness is in a way a good thing for many of us.

I begin to see the reasoning behind the requirements of many church orders that force aspirants to go into almost complete seclusion for a time. Turns your thoughts in upon yourself—not always, I find, a pleasant business—shows up some unexpected weaknesses and unexpected strengths. Too much of it would be bad enough—but a bit don't hurt.

◆ ◆ ◆

I mentioned propaganda a while ago. Should have included the fact that in addition to German newspapers and news-broadcasts, we have two magazines issued especially for English-speaking people.

These are "Signal"—a special magazine which is a rather conscious copy of "Look" but which lacks greatly in materials. Its effort seems devoted to showing Germany Army strength, German defenses, and an effort to humanize the German Reich and people; making these things seem attractive. It is printed beautifully in color on seemingly good-grade paper stock.

The other is an English version of "Der Adler" (The Eagle)—a sort of news-magazine, printed in rotogravure, and devoted almost exclusively to the Army, the Luftwaffe and its activities, strengths and potentialities.

In addition to these, there is "OK—The Overseas Kid", a weekly newspaper (four pages, tabloid size) edited in Berlin and purportedly issued exclusively for the benefit of American prisoners-of-war.

"OK" contains full translations of the German High Command communiques for the past week, some contributions (poems, articles, etc.) from POWs, and a great deal of material gleaned from American newspapers and radio broadcasts.

Most of the stuff that it prints from home is carefully selected to put home affairs in their worst light—almost all the items being devoted to strikes, labor troubles of all kinds, political arguments, criminal activities, etc. Almost any article or speech taking the U.S. to task for any shortage—like criticism in Congress of the Administration, or comments on the need for slum clearance—is sure of prominence in "OK".

Still, by careful reading between the lines, and always with a grain of salt, there is quite a bit of general information in all this.

"OK's" editor, who seems to be a German who spent considerable time in the States, doesn't give us credit for broad enough knowledge of our own country and conditions there to understand that these things are more or less normal, and not at all any sign of the decay of the nation or the political system under which it operates.

The Wrong Side of the Fence

There are also several illustrated German-language magazines. All these—like "Signal" and "Der Adler" are well printed, and rather obviously government subsidized, since they speak in the same tone, and carry almost no advertising.

September 19, 1944
Sagan

Despite the favorable look of the Western front, our own camp command is being wisely prudent, trying for maximum re-distribution and maximum utilization of available supplies, to see that everyone has nearly sufficient clothing to keep warm in the colder weather ahead. Boys who have received clothing from home are turning in extra socks and other clothes for redistribution.

Another air-raid alarm about midnight, somewhere north and east of us. We could hear the rumble of explosions.

Aside from the obvious stories of heroism here, there are several others that need to be told, I think.

Major one, to me, is that centering around the achievement of making life livable here by nothing more than the good old American virtues of grit and self-reliance. The conversion of worthless tin cans into useable implements; construction of tools from sticks of wood; the "make-do" that converts wood scraps and cardboard into passable stage sets for our shows; the publication of camp newspapers; activities of the band—these and many more are things that should gladden the heart of anyone who fears for the future of the nation.

Psychologically, there's another story. All these men, living so inescapably close together, as prisoners, with no variety, no diversion—and there hasn't been a single serious fight, and so far only one case of mental trouble.

From an organizational standpoint too, there's quite a story. This camp is almost without precedent in our military history, and many a step taken by its leaders has been entirely pioneering. These men have done a first-class job, a job that is a story in itself.

And the stories of escape attempts, the establishment and success of our school system, all these should be told, and at length. (See Appendix #2.)

September 22, 1944
Sagan

I have a feeling—and it seems to be backed up by events in the news as we get it from the Germans—that something big is going on now in the West. It is backed up by the lack of OKW comment.

As I've said before, we receive German news broadcasts in four major doses daily—at 10 A.M., 1:30 P.M., 3 P.M. and 4 P.M., and occasionally later in the day. The 10:30, 1:30 and 3 P.M. broadcasts are made in a manner that indicates they are summaries for the people at large, while the 4 P.M. broadcast is a direct OKW release, given carefully, with all town-names carefully

September, 1944

spelled out, apparently for copying and posting by newspapers and at Army posts.

Well, four days ago, OKW reported Allied paratroop and glider landings in Northern and middle Holland—around Arnhem—and did not claim to have been able to mop up these troops immediately, as has previously been claimed.

Three days ago, the 10 A.M. broadcast was a very hasty summary, saying almost nothing at all about any front, except that heavy fighting was going on on all sides. By the way—this is a recognized technique to prepare the way for damaging admissions later.

After the summary Tuesday morning, there were no further broadcasts at all that day.

Wednesday morning, again, there was only another hasty summary, making no specific mention of anything, saying that heavy fighting continued, particularly in middle Holland hinting that the Russians are on the move. And nothing more, and no other broadcasts until 4 P.M. This last devoted itself entirely to tales of heroic action of garrisons at St. Nazaire, Brest, and elsewhere in the West, and little else; another technique which permits the usual broadcast to go on at scheduled time, without necessitating admissions.

Thursday, all the regular broadcasts were given, all reported heavy fighting, none mentioned any specific localities, excepting that Brest had fallen. And today the same—except the statement that the Russ are now using 50 divisions in their attack on the East.

It all adds up, we think, to some very large development. We'll see, shortly, how well we read the signs.

September 24, 1944
Sagan

Nothing doing yet on the news front. Looking over what I've written in the last few items, I recognize symptoms of the old malady—lack of news and poor weather. Though we know the end is coming, the lack of food—news—to feed it makes our morale skid downward.

Optimists who, last week, were willing to bet the war would end in a matter of days have started to hedge their bets. Silly, but we couldn't help it, betting on the end. Personally, I hold to the Nov. 1 date.

Study in psychology: When we returned from Appel tonight, we found a neatly-printed card on the table in each combine. One side of the card was a facsimile of the cover of a British handbook on guerilla fighting, superimposed with quotes from it which are supposed to illustrate the complete abandonment of legal warfare by the Allies.

The other side was devoted to a lengthy warning to us not to attempt to escape, since we may then be considered guerrillas or saboteurs.

As the weather gets colder and our sports program dwindles down, our activities—physical—dwindle more and more to nothing but walking the perimeter of the compound. Round and round we go—three times makes a little under two miles—always within the barbed wire, always under the scrutiny of the guards.

But it's exercise that doesn't take too much out of a man (we must consider that, on short rations) and almost the only place where we can carry on conversations and discussions without fear of eavesdropping.

To provide other diversions, we have managed to fill our "theater" almost nightly with a series of lectures, band programs, plays, etc.

In addition to a class or two that I'm attending, I've set myself the task of catching up on my reading—picking up and reading whatever is available in the works of authors I should know—Galsworthy, Masefield, Hervey Allen; and titles I should know, as "A Tree Grows In Brooklyn". I may not have such a chance again for years.

Find myself turning more and more to this writing as a relief—sort of unloading my thoughts on someone (a task Ann used to undertake at home to her great credit and probably utter boredom). What started out to be a record for myself, and partially a long letter for Ann, has become instead a safety-valve for me.

September 26, 1944
Sagan

A cold miserable day—raining and unpleasant, impossible to get comfortably warm, even in bed under the covers.

Good thing the soil here is sandy, else we'd be hip-deep in mud by this time, with all the moisture that's been coming down from the sky. This time of year, you can have this country for all of me, though the short summer is pleasant enough.

The news too, has been continuing very slow—still no place-names or definite locations of fighting. But we know there is a major battle going on on both sides.

However, the combination of little news and dismal weather haven't helped any. We are like the fairy princess—we wait only to be rescued, but can't do much to speed or aid the rescue itself.

Taught Gomez and Cole some chess tonight. Haven't played it myself for some time, but was fun. Also have taught Post bridge (with considerable help).

Tomorrow, Cole and Gomez are due to reciprocate with some lessons in pinochle.

Improving my time, as is obvious.

September 29, 1944
Sagan

Let this go for three days for various reasons—among them the fact that the weather has continued miserable and cold, making activity of any kind unpleasant.

September, 1944

Apparently my hunch about the imminence of a news-break was premature—nothing has happened to justify it. In fact, the withdrawal of the troops landed in Northern Holland has had a damping effect.

Find we are all becoming conversationalists on only one subject—when and how we get out of here.

New purge came in a couple of days ago, and among them was Nick Gettino, who went through navigation school with me. He tells me a couple others of our class are down, too. Seems a long time ago.

Haven't been feeling too well lately, hard to sleep, because of the cold and headaches. Dunno what's the matter, but not serious, anyway.

September 30, 1944
Sagan

End of another month here—and we've been down three months. Incredible. The days slide into each other faster and faster, receding behind us like fence-posts viewed from the rear of a rushing train.

But, by my own calculations at least, we are entering our last 30 days here. Admit I haven't anything more to base this opinion on than mere conjecture and my own brand of logic. But I cling to it.

We've had two more purges this week—18 and 15 men—both from hospitals. The Germans are apparently trying to clear their hospitals of any and all men who are able to get about by themselves. No sign of Dave yet, though.

These men bring tales of how the POW's were treated (by our own Army) after their release from Rumania. Seem to have been well handled, and generous. Leaves and promotions for all.

Hope we are handled as expeditiously. We'll need a return to something at least approaching normalcy for awhile, before trying anything else.

Often commented on the fact that Army friendships are often so very facile. You meet a man, live with him—and then one day orders come, and you go one way and he another. And in a short time neither of you can recall the other's name, and must search memory diligently to visualize mannerisms and experience.

Listening-in to conversations here suggests an answer. Fact is that all of us have only one thing really in common—our Army service. It is one thing that we can discuss in general, and all take an interest in.

All our other life—before we were uprooted and thrown together thus—is a book in which only we are really interested. When we discuss these things, our difference in age, experience, schooling, family background, become immediately apparent. But when we speak of Army experience, we are on common ground.

Chapter 5

♦

October, 1944

October 2, 1944
Sagan

It's not yet 8 P.M., and we're indoors, lights on, barracks-shutters closed—and I'm feeling somewhere near warm for the first time.

As has been usual for the past week or so, it has been raining, with resultant cold and discomfort.

In the Army generally—even in the Air Corps—the weather is of much less concern to the individual than in civilian life. As a civilian, one dodges the weather—hugs the radiator and the dry room, plays with iced drinks and electric fans, dresses (or undresses) to accommodate himself to the elements. One can even await more suitable weather to accomplish whatever must be done.

But in the Army, a man learns to accept the weather as an inanimate object—something that's there. Whether it's wet or dry, hot or cold, windy or calm—the war won't wait. So a soldier grumbles, but does what must be done regardless of the weather.

Here, though, we're between the two extremes. We haven't sufficient clothes or means of making ourselves comfortable at all. And we have no urgent tasks to perform, either.

So bad days keep us indoors, make us miserable and glum, contribute to low spirits.

October 5, 1944
Sagan

The last two days have been beautiful—clear and warm—and we have been duly grateful. But the nights are bitterly cold. The two meager German-issued blankets most of us have are completely inadequate against this biting, damp cold, and most of us have taken to going to bed with a good part of our few clothes on. And even so, I, for one, have had difficulty sleeping. Might be a tough winter.

Yesterday brought three announcements on the grim side too—or rather, one slightly ludicrous and two grim ones.

October, 1944

First was the announcement that two cases of diphtheria have been discovered. This is, of course, terribly serious. Crowded so closely together any kind of an epidemic would sweep this camp like the "Black Death" of the Middle Ages. Inadequately clothed and fed as we are, we have little resistance to this sort of thing, I fear.

The camp command (German) immediately quarantined the barracks where the cases developed, set aside a latrine for the men there, called off theater programs until further notice. This all being done at our—not the German—instigation.

And then, to top off, came the announcement that the Germans will increase the complement of the five camps here by 4,000 men. Apparently for reasons of economy of men and materials, they are planning to clean out the camps at Barth and elsewhere, concentrating all here, we understand.

The crowding is going to be really terrific. They plan to make all our bunks triple-deckers, and crowd 225 men into the already bulging barracks. Two hundred and twenty-five in a barracks that should not house more than 70! And in winter, with no heat. A cough will travel quickly.

No wonder we get a bit hot under the collar when we remember that at home POW's live in steam-heated barracks, with hot showers, decent beds, ample food.

The third announcement was anti-climactic. We are no longer to be allowed to keep our beloved tin cans, out of which we have made so many dishes, tin pans, covers, etc. It seems a Gestapo agent was here, and got scared we might use the cans to shore up tunnels, or even build a tank or something to aid in escape. Which, of course, is entirely true.

So each evening we'll have to put out the tin cans in a carefully counted pile, accounting for each one, before the Germans will permit us to get new Red Cross parcels.

October 9, 1944
Sagan

Raining and miserable again—but the last three days were decent and sunshiny, so we're not too bad off right now.

And the news is good! OKW admits advances near Aachen, but big gains by the Russ in Hungary. And from the stories some of our boys tell of the treatment they received there, it should do the Hungarians good.

Anyway, my prediction still looks good.

We are at present involved in a barracks-wide bridge tournament—another scheme to keep us busy, now that we must stay indoors so much. We've gotten up to 17 teams, and so will each play 16 games. Highest total scorers to win a carton of cigarettes.

Interest is amazing—always surprising here how completely a man can sink himself into something as simple as a card game—and I for one am hav-

The Wrong Side of the Fence

ing my fill of playing. At the moment, with Cy Eatinger as partner, I'm up near the top. Damned good playing too, all in all.

Most of us are angry over letters from home commenting on how well cared for we are. It's all to the good that the folks are assured we are safe and well—but what kind of propaganda are they getting to think that we all have cozy rooms, comfortable beds and chairs, shows, etc.?

Practically everything we have we've been forced to make for ourselves, without tools and with a great deal of effort—and that goes for chairs as well as everything else. Our beds are straw—no, wood-shaving sacks, hard as rocks; our plates tin cans; our toilets nothing but outhouses. And there are many men here who have been behind the wire for over a year, and have never been taken outside the camp—while at home POW's get into town, have access to a real PX, and decent living conditions to boot.

October 11, 1944
Sagan

Well, the Big Push has apparently started.

Two days ago, OKW said the Allies had opened up a heavy offensive on all fronts—U.S. and British on the West and Russians on the East and Southeast.

By today, the Russ are almost in Memel and well into Hungary, while the Allies grind away at the Siegfried line at Aachen, Metz, Belfort. To date, although testifying to the weight of the attacks and air pounding, OKW reports no great progress on the West.

But we expect things to be slow for a few days on the West—the defenses are obviously deep and desperately manned. But I still like the looks of the Nov. 1 date.

Maybe I'm being foolish about that prediction—I don't know. A lot of the older men, inured by many spurts and recessions in hopes, have adopted a pessimistic attitude on the general theory that anything good that comes must be "gravy" thereby. And I know I'll be downcast if it don't pan out.

But all the logic I seem to be able to muster points to a near end. Time, as always, will tell.

Something else to be considered too is the possibility of trouble here. No telling what sort of a panic might excite the local populace, or what orders the more fanatical Nazis might try to carry out in an attempt to hold us as hostages. To be considered, although there isn't much we can do.

◆ ◆ ◆

Should have mentioned that three weeks, ago, two of the lads in the combine—Applegate and Kramer—offered to take over all cooking duties for the combine, on the theory that men cooking steadily could do more towards conserving food than we can do if we change cooks each week. They've been doing marvelously well.

October, 1944

And at least one of my predictions has come true—that I'd never cook here.

Germans started triple-decking the bunks in the barracks today, in preparation for the coming influx of men. We're to sleep in tiers, as in a slave-galley. Another reason it is best to hope for a quick ending.

Fall has really arrived. Walking the perimeter last night I smelt leaves burning—which made me homesick. And the few trees we have that are not pine—mostly silver beech and oak—have turned quickly, their reds and browns startling against the sombre green of the encircling pines.

October 13, 1944
Sagan

Air raid alarm again two nights ago. Getting to be a lot of them.

Also, a lot of mail coming in—some for men who came in only a week or so before we did. As I've said, I really have not expected to receive any mail while here—but now I begin to have some hopes. Only one letter would be needed—just so I know things are alright at home. But so far, none of us has received mail.

As the war itself seems to grow closer to an end, I think I note the German guards here growing more affable—eager to try out what English they know, ask us where we live, how life goes in America. (See Appendix #5.)

An amazing thing is that we have long had the custom of shouting "Tallyho" whenever a guard or a ferret enters the barracks—the cry following them while they're inside, and serving as a warning to all.

Don't believe they've ever figured out what it means, though. And lately, the guards have been entering the buildings shouting "Tallyho" themselves, smiling broadly the while.

Went to work on a stump-pulling detail yesterday, along with most of the barracks. As I've said, this camp-site was once a pine forest, and some thousands of stumps were left in the ground after construction.

Our fuel shortage may become really serious, so camp authorities proposed to the Germans that we be permitted to pull the stumps for use as firewood. They agreed—of course we're clearing the land for them and saving coal—and we were glad to do the work.

As officers, we cannot be made to work, but we don't mind at all. Something to do.

October 15, 1944
Sagan

We've just finished dinner—and for once I am stuffed, replete, comatose.

The dinner was larger than any I have had since I've been in Germany, and was accomplished by dint of heavy stinting during the week. But it was worth it, just to eat one's fill for a change.

The Wrong Side of the Fence

Occasion was worthy—Pat Kelly has become the father of a girl, his second. The child was born August 12, but he only found out about it last week—peculiarly enough through a letter received by another inmate whose wife knows Pat's wife. A fine way to discover you're a father. But not far out of the ordinary in Kriegie life.

Anyway, in honor of the event, we all put on our best clothes, sat down at the table in full regalia, plus neckties, like officers and gentlemen, for once.

A thing to remember, and cause memories. For good food engendered memory of other and more varied foods. Which of course brought thoughts of back home.

Went to Sunday Church service today—as I have most Sundays since arrival. Not that I have any great religious fervor, but attendance puts a period to the week, lifts Sunday out of the monotony of the days here, sets it apart. And, although Lt. Daniels sounds not at all like Dr. Hartley at home, the service and the hymns are the same. So it's another touch of home.

News continues good—Russ closing in on Memel, Riga, Belgrade, Budapest. Germans admit evacuating the Balkans and Greece. On the West, though, things grind slowly. Maybe too slowly.

Only 16 days left to make my prediction come true. Funny—I can savor getting out of here, just as I savored the thought of getting a commission. But when I did get my commission, I found it rather curt—even flat. Suppose getting out of here might be just as matter of fact.

Star-gazing last night—unaccountably clear (surely a good omen!), and thinking of the difficulty I had learning the stars back in navigation school. But they're old friends now, and good to see them.

October 18, 1944
Sagan

Red letter day for me. I've gotten word from home!

Not to me directly, but one from Mother to Col. Spivey. Very much like Kelly's finding out about his newest child from another. But a tremendous relief to me.

It seems that the folks were notified that I was missing in action about July 4, and then had to wait a whole month—until August 2—until they were told that I was a prisoner. I regret this delay more than I can possibly say, though of course there is nothing that can be done about it.

Anyway, from the time of notification until the date of the letter (Sept. 12) they had no further word, though I wrote July 7 from Wetzlar. And then, in a Red Cross bulletin, Mother saw a picture of POW's at this camp, thought one of them was me (it wasn't) and wrote the Colonel forthwith.

I know Mother—she'd write Roosevelt or anyone else, if she thought it'd help my situation.

But the letter was tremendous to me—it implied that Ann and the folks were OK. It shocked me in that I thought they had received some mail from me

October, 1944

by that time—but I hope that by now they have received some. And it gave Post and Cole some idea that their people at least know they are safe.

I can't quite describe what I felt when I saw that letter—but a phrase of something I read once, somewhere, kept running through my head—"the smell of well-remembered things." Mother's firm, flowing writing, her stationery, are certainly well-remembered.

Somehow the note made home suddenly seem more real and alive—not quite the academic and far-away thing it has seemed lately.

I'm slowly becoming convinced that what OKW called a "major attack" on the 11th wasn't that at all. Seems to me we could have done more damage and gotten further in this drive with the forces at our disposal, if it were a major move.

Looks more as if the move around Aachen and in Holland are further jockeyings for position, prior to the main move. But things better get moving if we're to get out of here by the time my prediction is up.

Funny, how when hope is all you have to live by, you clutch at anything to bolster it. I've never taken much stock in dreams or the portents that may be drawn from them. And yet, last night I dreamt I would receive mail. And look what happened. The same night I dreamt I was flying again, in a small plane, with Hamilton.

It's easy to manufacture assurance out of that—if I was flying, I must have been free. Silly to count it at all—but who knows?

October 20, 1944
Sagan

Another rainy, cold day, third in a row, all of which goes to prove the cliché that Germany's weather is "nine months of winter, three months of bad weather". Worst of it being that it's impossible to get warm unless one is in bed.

News remains good, but progress is so slow! So slow! My notes show that the Allies reached the outskirts of Aachen on Sept. 17—and finally, two days ago, the town was completely encircled. A whole month! Of course we realize that the war has other purposes than our rescue, and weightier matters than our fate are in the balance. But we have no choice but to sit and wait—and that's the hardest part of the business.

Listened to Himmler calling on the people for fanatical defense last night. I don't speak German, but from listening to their daily broadcasts, I find I'm increasingly able to follow the general drift of a German conversation.

Discovered trace of Santora today, in my periodic search for him and Dave. In a list of men who have passed through the big hospital at Obermasfeld, I found that Joe had left there July 28, bound for a convalescent hospital at Meininger. So he's OK. But no sign of Dave. He may still be at Obermasfeld, for all we know.

The Wrong Side of the Fence

October 22, 1944
Sagan

Been raining and drizzling all day. Indoors.

But a mercy tempers the situation. We lit the big Nuremberg stove in the barracks, with the altogether surprising result that the building has been at least livable all afternoon and most of the evening.

And the news picks up a bit. Russians are advancing at great rate across Hungary after a big breakthrough, similar breakthrough in East Prussia. And Aachen is now in our hands. Nov. 1 looks better—God! how I hope it's right!

Did a bit of checking yesterday (for the paper) and found that the Red Cross has shipped more than 580 tons of food into this camp from Jan. 1 to Sept. 1, to feed the 6360 Americans here. Think what a load that is off the German transport and supply services.

October 23, 1944
Sagan

Meant to write more last night, but the light is so bad in my bunk (we have one 60-watt bulb for the whole combine) and the table being occupied by no less than two bridge games, I found it impossible to go further and still save my eyesight.

So today opened, as usual, cloudy and dreary—but with good news, news that has gotten better all day. The Russ have made "deep" penetrations into East Prussia, says OKW; are advancing rapidly in Hungary; for the first time there is mention of fierce fighting in Central Slovakia (and the old Czech border is only 70 miles from us!) and apparently we and the British have opened up again along the entire Western front—although no material progress is mentioned there as yet.

Surprisingly, OKW now seems to be admitting penetrations and large-scale Allied activity as fast as they occur. Only explanation that occurs to me is the old political trick of getting in first with your side of a bad story, and an attempt to spur the people to that "fanatical resistance" the Nazi leaders have been calling for, by painting as black a picture as possible.

In any event, it appears that the significance I read the other day into the announcement that the English and Stalin were in conference was justified. Looks as if the Allies had held off long enough to make a final settlement before launching the all-out attack we've been expecting so long.

Hope this IS the attack.

Looking back on the entries I have made here in the past two weeks, I find what seems to be an undue emphasis on news. But it serves two purposes—first to emphasize our hunger and dependence on news to give point to our existence; second, I've found these notes to be a handy calendar of events. Our days are so monotonously the same that it becomes extremely difficult to remember just when a particular event took place.

October, 1944

Lot of personal parcels from home in again—though none for any of our combine or crew. And now that many have "capital" in the form of extra cigarettes and tobacco, poker games have started all over camp. Silly and childish it may be, but it's a form of excitement, and undeniably passes the gloomy days.

On something akin to this—I've been reading a collection of travel stories recently, and find that I appreciate a lot more fully the descriptions of hunger and privation. But always in the back of my mind is the thought that, although the adventurers' hardships may be many and great, they got into them of their own free will—which we did not—and they were at all times masters of their own fate—which we are not.

They don't, therefore, have my complete and unqualified sympathy.

New purge in two days ago—14 enlisted men, who had been picked up while in the hands of the French and Belgian underground. They say Gestapo sent them to Dachau, where they spent several weeks living in an open trench, before the Luftwaffe got them out, sent them here.

Some of the stories they tell about Dachau are disgusting—a wonder they were allowed to leave after seeing some of the things they speak of.

October 26, 1944
Sagan

Clear skies this afternoon, first in four days and a welcome change. News continues good on the Russ side, but the Allies on the West seem content with mopping up around Antwerp, and prods at the Siegfried Line.

Big day yesterday—two classes in the morning, bath (via tin bucket and pan) in the afternoon, attendance at the play "Arsenic and Old Lace" in the evening. To my unsophisticated eye and ear, the play was as well-produced and acted as any I've ever seen.

And, oh yes, a really superb cake, produced by Applegate—who is becoming a first-class pastry cook, despite all handicaps.

I had thought that in my Army career up to the time I got here, I'd learned to do without a great meal, and to make shift with a great deal more. But I learn every day. There are so many things that I must do without here, things that I always thought I must have, that I'm sure I'd be hard-pressed if some genie should offer me just one or two choices in things to do and eat.

For instance:

A hot bath, really hot, with limitless supplies of hot water, with all the time I want to sit and soak; a barber-shop shave and haircut with all the lotions and powders that go with it; fresh, clean, pressed clothes that are made to fit me alone; a real bed, with springs and a mattress; a comfortable chair to lounge in or read in; rugs on the floor; heat—real warmth, and I don't care if it comes from a radiator or fireplace, just so it's clean and constant; good light to work or read by; a decent bathroom with a washbowl and good light, and a real toilet that flushes and doesn't smell; privacy—to sleep or read or walk alone if I wish it, to choose my companions as fancy dictates, rather than fortune; diversion in the form of movies, radio, play—what I choose; news.

As to food, I have no particular choice or favorite. I think what I most want is to have enough of any food so that when I leave the table I feel satisfied. Of course, I can and do conjure up endless dishes I've eaten and would like to eat again—but I think the main thing right now is quantity, not quality.

And, to top off what is only a meager list—two more. To see and be with Ann, and to have work, real work, to do again.

That business of work is one that interests me—never realized how much it does to give a man's life some meaning, to make time pass, to stimulate the mind and body.

For here we have no work, except what we make for ourselves, and we are very often caught up in the realization that it is pointless and meaningless, leading us nowhere. We go to bed at night because it is the thing to do—not because we are mentally or physically tired. We vegetate very literally, punctuating and aiming our day at meals, at Appels, at necessary trips to the toilet—and to bedtime.

But I haven't said what I started out to say. Which is that I—who considered himself among those hardest hit when rationing of sugar went into effect at home, have learned to drink coffee and tea without sweetening (since our ration of $1/2$ pound of sugar per two weeks doesn't go far); to husband my small candy ration (six squares every two weeks) so that it lasts me a week; to take only one bath a week at considerable discomfort; to confine myself to five slices of black bread a day; to wearing and sleeping in long underwear and anything else in the way of clothes I can put my hands on; to being absolutely without contact with home.

October 30, 1944
Sagan

Writing this in the camp library—which has been made out of an end of one of our two cookhouses—the only really warm spot I've been able to find.

Weather has turned cold in the last four days, bitterly cold under the dull grey of these unfriendly skies—and it seems impossible to seal up or heat up our barracks.

So I—and as many others as can crowd in—have taken to spending a good part of the day in the library. It's salutary, too. In the period of the past year, with the cooperation of the YMCA and the omnipresent Red Cross, we have built up a considerable list of reference works—including some volumes on journalism. So I keep warm, and try to learn a few things about my profession—hereto a matter of practical experience to me, rather than theory.

Only thing that bothers me greatly is the strain on my eyes—I find I'm reading constantly in bad light, for lack of anything else to do.

October, 1944

Almost hate to dwell on the news any more. Not that it is bad, but it seems to offer so little encouragement to our hopes of an early release from this place. All that we armchair (or rather, four-legged stool) strategists can do is conjecture, and our conjecturing doesn't seem to come out right most of the time.

As nearly as we can figure it out right now, for whatever it may be worth, it appears that the delay is mostly political and not military. Seems to be dictated by the Allies' desire to come to the peace-table with plans ready, rather than anything else. That, and the possibility that the Germans may yet lay down their arms, without too much bloodshed.

But, whatever the reasons for the delay, never were more fervent hopes expressed so unanimously before, as by this group of men who have so much to gain by the ending.

A few hopes and conjecture—a fine contribution towards winning a war! But it's all we can do. And my prediction of Nov. 1 is glimmering very faintly now.

Spoke to Col. Spivey today to thank him for his kindness in regard to mother's letter. He told me he received many similar notes—all kindly and promptly answered, I know.

Chapter 6

♦

November, 1944

November 2, 1944
Sagan

Well, I note the date, and also that I'm not such a hot prophet. At least insofar as specific dates are concerned.

Can't quite figure out what's going on. As is of course quite obvious. But don't understand what's going on in the West. The Allies have obviously assembled large forces, which are ready and waiting—but waiting for what? For the Germans to give up? For negotiations to be completed?

I suppose we may never know. But whatever it is, I'm satisfied as to the result. Anyway, my prediction's failure cost me a "D" bar—to Eatinger.

Not to say my optimism is less. It is not. I still expect to see the end of this business soon. But it's only seven weeks to Christmas, and things go so slowly. And the days and weeks since I was shot down begin to slip by at a terrifying rate.

Another 62 men came in today—we have now 160 in the barracks—and they were greeted by a thin sunshine. The sunshine was occasion for me to get a long-postponed washing of clothes. And then it rained in the afternoon, which has made the problem of getting my things dry a serious one.

At the library the other day, I read a translation of Goebbels' latest speech, which seems to be a complete reversal of Himmler's demand for "fanatical resistance". Goebbels asked only that Germans continue to fight for an "honorable peace", rather than fight to the death. Interesting.

We're on half-rations now, and rumor has it that we'll be on quarter-rations in two weeks. But the Germans have unexpectedly increased potato and kohlrabi rations. So we may make out alright after all.

Still no mail from home—but my thoughts are always there.

November 4, 1944
Sagan

A dull, dreary day again, and I believe I've hit a new low in my hopes. I think it's time I confess it to myself at least—I'm no longer able to believe

November, 1944

anything I've figured out about the end of this business. I'd thought we might see the end this month, even—all my poor logic points to it. But I can't say that I really believe that.

Nothing seems to be happening on the fronts at all. The Russ are obviously slowing down again—despite activities in Hungary and the Balkans. And our boys on the West haven't moved in nearly two months. It looks as if something has gone wrong with the plan or schedule, or both, and the Allies seem content to settle down to a winter-long waiting game. Which would be bad, because any real evidence that the drives have been stopped will fall right in with the Nazis' claims that they can and have stopped the best efforts of their enemies. Such a thing, if a fact, would strengthen them immeasurably.

Does this sound callous—heartless—with no regard for the men who must fight to bring an end and effect our release? Particularly since I sit in safety?

It is all that, and I know it. But I can't look at this disinterestedly. My own desperate longing to go home, to be with Ann, to do a thousand things I cannot do because I am not free—colors everything I think or do. I've been reading back over this stuff and find it dull and dreary—and rightly so. This is a dull and dreary life.

And the prospect of months more of this is almost terrifying to me. Not that I won't survive it—we all will.

But months more of living behind the wire, months of renewed and dashed hopes, of endless and pointless conjecture, of abortive attempts at study, of walking the same perimeter track, seeing the same faces, living in the same endless, stupid circle—what a prospect for a group of men in the prime of life!

Maybe it does some good to put it down on paper. Maybe, years from now, I'll look back on this time with complacency, even amusement. But not now.

Added a new accomplishment—making quilts. Very simple, you double up a blanket, fill the space between the folds with straw and old newspapers, and sew it up. Surprisingly warm, too.

Band show last night—excellent. Hard to realize that those boys making so smoothly with the jive were engaged in grimmer business so short a time ago.

November 7, 1944
Sagan

Election day back home, with all that it means, with parades and headlines and excitement and sitting up all night to hear how things are coming out—in fact, the things we believe we came over here to help preserve.

To us it doesn't mean much directly, since we can't vote, and since most of us have been so long away that the issues are not clear at all. And, since there is a six-hour time difference between New York and Sagan, we won't even get any results until late tomorrow, it then. But we'll know, because the Germans are watching keenly. They would like to see Roosevelt defeated.

The Wrong Side of the Fence

So speculation is rife, and I believe that if a poll were taken now, the President would win here, hands down.

Looking back on what I wrote about the war the other day, I find myself in a much better frame of mind, and inclined to feel that what I wrote was something in the nature of a bad tempered outburst.

I think by now that I've reconciled myself to the idea that further time must be spent here, since it now appears that unless some attack is made shortly—or some unexpected collapse occurs—it will be several months before the war is at an end.

In a way, that is just as well. Much as I want to get out of here, I think I would rather stay a bit longer, if by so doing I could somehow ensure a more clean-cut, decisive ending that would preclude this sort of thing happening again.

I am not so sanguine as to believe that the world can be rendered permanently peaceful at the cessation of this war, but I can hope that enough can come out of this war to at least point the way towards equitable relationships between the nations and people of the world.

And if, to achieve that end, I must sacrifice some more of my not completely invaluable time—it's not so much of a contribution on my part.

◆ ◆ ◆

Should mention that Timoshenka's last brood—once cute—have now become a problem.

They are more than half-grown now, and the compound seems to be swarming with them. They get into everything and in everybody's way, being privileged characters and knowing it.

Kelly got a food parcel today—an event I should mention.

Like the others—Applegate, Eatinger, Bascom—who have received similar parcels, he has thrown all but a small store into the common pot. "Gash" we call it.

This is a great boon to us all—has kept us newer men in smokes and other essentials. And the addition of condiments, flours, etc., makes an immense difference in rations.

Wrote Ann night before last, and included Christmas greetings—the words not covering half the sentiment. But I begin to doubt —as noted—that I'll be able to deliver them in person.

Weather has been mercifully dry for the past two days—mercifully for me, with my shoes now leaking very badly, and no facilities for repair or replacement. And news is slow, still clearing Antwerp on the West, Russ about in Budapest.

November 9, 1944
Sagan

A brief note this time, just to note the news and a slight upswing in optimism.

November, 1944

First, German radio made one brief mention of the fact that President Roosevelt has been re-elected. They don't seem happy about it.

Other note, on which we are yet reserving judgment, is a considerable fuss OKW is raising about what it calls a large-scale attack by Americans between Nancy and Metz.

We reserve judgment because OKW miscalled a major attack only recently (near Aachen), and we want to see if it is actually that, or only position fighting. Opinion here is agreed that we have only two chances to leave here now before Spring or early Summer: Some sort of a deal between the Germans and the Allies, or a major attack.

So we watch this attack, and wait, with plenty of emotion.

November 12, 1944
Sagan

Armistice Day has come and gone—my second great holiday in captivity. It was a hollow occasion for us in a way, but we marked it with a memorial service in the theater—which included the expressed opinion (in which I heartily concur) that the next Armistice Day we'll mark here will be for the end of the war, not the last one.

And the usual digression on the news.

Not a digression, really, since news is almost our main business here. Anyway, the drive around Metz and Nancy still continues, but with no very startling results as yet. It has made some advances—passed Chateau Salins—but nothing major. Of course, even if it is not the main drive (and it might be, since we've finally cleared Antwerp and its approaches) it has to grind through some very heavy defenses before fast action can be expected.

But we're still reserving judgment. Meanwhile, on the East and South, the Russians seem to be confining themselves to mopping up and consolidation of their current gains. Which must be a major job in itself.

I've taken up a desultory study of philosophy. I've the chance, and, Lord knows, the time, and it's a subject of which I know very little. Don't know if I'll finish it, but it's in line with my prison-born idea that a man's enjoyment of life is in direct ration to his knowledge of life.

Food situation gives promise of easing, communications between here and Switzerland, and Switzerland and the sea, having been restored, we are told. However, the heating problem gets worse—been getting steadily colder, and no coal.

Just one world-shaking problem after another.

November 14, 1944
Sagan

New purge came in last night, and with it startling news:
Post is to be a father.

The Wrong Side of the Fence

Like Kelly's news and others, it's a peculiar way to be informed of such an intimate thing as that, but it shows how things happen here. We've had no mail.

In the purge last night was a man who hails from Post's home town (Pendleton, Ind.), and this man—Lt. Bill Bunch—by sheer coincidence is engaged to a close friend of Post's wife. And it happened that four months ago, while we were still getting adjusted to life here, and while they at home knew only that we were missing, Bunch had spoken to Irene (Mrs. Post). She was well, he said, and full of hope.

There is no describing how we felt on hearing this, since we all knew Irene. Of course, I can't pretend to say how Bob himself felt, though I can imagine.

We celebrated the news tonight with an extra can of Spam for dinner.

◆ ◆ ◆

As I check over each new purge that comes in, looking for Dave and other friends, I find myself getting jealous, silly as that may seem.

For I feel a bit cheated in this war—seem doomed in this, as in so many other things, to the role of spectator, rather than participant.

I know it's supreme foolishness to argue with the Fates, but somehow I feel as if I hadn't had a fair chance to see more of the war, experience more of what so many others are going through and have gone through. And that feeling is pointed up as each new group comes in. For instance, in the last lot was a man whose navigation school class was 44-8, a class that hadn't started at San Marcos when I graduated. And yet, he had been on more combat missions than I, had seen more of the war.

Of course I know, and am thankful, that I am lucky to be alive and well. And also that I might very well have completed that last mission and several more—and then ended up not nearly so fortunate.

But I'm far enough away from the occurrence now to feel as if I'd been unfairly treated, somehow. Which is manifestly foolish, but I can't seem to help it.

Bascom, by the way, hit the jackpot in the way of parcels from home today—receiving five in all, three cigarette parcels, and two others packed with food and clothing.

We all benefitted, as usual, and Bascom is a rich man.

November 16, 1944
Sagan

First snow of the winter started last night and continued all day today—a mean half-snow, half-rain, just such a miserable bit of weather as we used to curse (but dodge) at home this time of year.

With no sidewalks or streets, our world became a sodden, ugly mess, through which we slop dispiritedly, confining ourselves to the damp, smoky barracks and reading, for lack of anything else to do.

November, 1944

Normally, I've been in the habit of walking ten or twelve times around the compound—a distance of three or five miles—daily. But in such weather it's hopeless to try. My shoes are now so badly worn that I am practically through the soles, and my feet get wet almost immediately I set foot outside the door.

Had an unexpected treat last night—the arrival of the movie "The Spoilers" with Marlene Dietrich and Randolph Scott. Very old, and the sound track very bad. But I had forgotten how a movie can take you out of yourself—for two hours I was out of this camp completely.

November 19, 1944
Sagan

Must mention the news first tonight, because it's important, I believe.

In addition to the drives I have mentioned, the Allies, day before yesterday, opened up what seems to be a general offensive along the entire Western front, notably at Aachen and below Baccarat in the Belfort Gap.

These actions now have progressed satisfactorily all along the line, according to OKW admissions (which speak of really heavy battles)—the front at Aachen widening in three days to cover 70 kilometers and going Eastward seven or eight miles. Other fronts show steady, grinding, but sure progress.

And as usual, I find my spirits going up and my morale with them—as with the whole camp. We are cautious, now, about letting our emotions and our hopes go—there have been too many disappointments—but this does so look as if it IS the big drive. For I cannot conceive that such actions as this now appears to be would be launched only as a diversion or a program to cut down German strength; nor that such a drive would be launched without sufficient backing to carry it through.

In any event, though I wouldn't bet on it, mind you—things are looking up.

Sometimes I read over this seemingly endless list of prognostications and news-notes and realize that part of the reason for them is my own wish to appear to myself and to anyone else who might read these notes as an unusually wise analyst. That is partially true. Though I must also admit that the notes themselves don't bear out the wisdom of my judgment.

But another reason is our general absorption in just such speculation. It forms the core of all our thinking, of almost all our conversation. For we have no past and no present here—only a future. And that future can't begin until the war ends.

Food situation brighter with the arrival of what must amount to tons of potatoes in the past few days.

Despite the rains, the Germans are working feverishly to store the spuds against the coming hard freeze, I suppose. They store them by having the Russ prisoners dig long trenches—about two feet deep and three wide—which are lined with straw, filled with potatoes, and the whole covered with another layer of straw, pine branches, and dirt.

The Wrong Side of the Fence

We have discovered virtues of potatoes as a dietary factor.

Food picture is still odd, to say the least. As I may have mentioned previously, the whole camp has been steadily saving out a proportion of non-perishable foods (chocolate, cheese, prunes, etc.) as a reserve supply for possible emergencies.

Now comes an order (from the Germans) that we may not have more than one day's supply of food on hand. They are apparently afraid that such a portable food supply may make us dangerous, potentially. But it's a real problem to us. Don't know as yet what's to be done about it.

November 21, 1944
Sagan

Raining again tonight, but warmer. Slept last night without socks on for the first time in some weeks.

We've been assured by the Germans that, at least for some time, we won't get any more men into the camp. They've finished a new compound at Bellaria (some five miles North of us) where they will send new prisoners for a time.

If true, it will be a mercy—we are already over the 180 mark in some barracks, which is a rough situation indeed.

November 23, 1944
Sagan

And the news continues good. So good, that I think our chances of seeing this Christmas (only four weeks away!) under the aegis of the United States rather than that of Germany grows hourly brighter. What a Christmas gift that would be!

The French army, having made a breakthrough near the Swiss border, has turned Northeastward, and is moving swiftly towards cutting off the Germans in the Vosges—being already North of Mulhausen and having reached the Rhine. Patton's army continues to move Eastward, one arm of its pincer around the anchor at Metz being already East of Saarbrucken. The British in Holland seem to be increasing their pressure, and the apparently heavy action around Aachen goes on.

This <u>must</u> be the final battle—the Germans must be throwing everything they have left into this attempt to stop the clock. And I don't believe they can stop it.

The wave of new optimism in our midst is measurable by the daily increase in the crowd that clusters around the OKW loudspeaker during news broadcasts.

Been engaged recently in an engineering project of a sort. As I've mentioned, walking the perimeter of the compound has been almost our sole exercise.

November, 1944

But the perimeter track itself is badly sunken in many spots, and becomes impossible after one of the almost daily rains. So we have been working for some days with shovels and sand to level the track off, and raise it in some places. Busy, busy, busy.

Last night Tom Mulligan, Ron Delaney, Sid Shore and I gave an open-forum discussion on journalism, for some 100 interested men. Was fun, find I don't mind public speaking at all.

Been doing a lot of talking about the G.I. Bill of Rights—about which we know only what driblets the newer purges have brought in. We're all convinced of one thing, though, and that is that the educational provisions are good.

We are all convinced that the day of the jack-of-all-trades is long gone, and that the day when a man must really know his trade has arrived. And specialists in what most of the younger men here know exclusively—aviation—will be plentiful after the war.

Perhaps it's as well it is not given to us to see ahead. Had I known when I started that I'd go even this far with this diary, it would have been far worse than it has been, waiting for the time to pass.

But it shows one of my earlier statements to be true—time does pass, and swiftly.

November 26, 1944
Sagan

The news again: our armies, spearheaded by the French have reached Strasbourg (two days ago) and it may be the breakthrough we've been praying for. Surely if an advance can be made up the Rhine Valley from there, it need not go very far to make the German Westwall positions untenable. Hope glows brighter again.

We've been eating heartily (for once) this week. Complying with orders to reduce our reserve food supplies, but will try to hold out one week's reserve, in spite of the Germans. No telling what may happen to our sources, and the Germans very obviously aren't prepared to increase their allotment to us if need arises. Had pies and extra fruit and cheese rations. And our stomachs, used to thin fare for so long, are reacting unexpectedly to the increase.

Weather has been holding up pretty well of late, not too cold and enough gap between rains to permit some walking again. As a result, I've developed some huge blisters on my feet—the result of wearing borrowed shoes that are much too big for me. My own being hopelessly cracked and worn.

Propaganda note: "Signal", "OK" and the German papers in general are sounding the tocsin in unison.

They no longer speak of victory at all, but devote themselves to dire pictures of a postwar, communist-run Europe, that will be chaos if the Germans are not there to supervise it.

The Wrong Side of the Fence

November 28, 1944
Sagan

We're preparing for a major celebration to take place day after tomorrow—Thanksgiving Day.

It sounds like a hollow mockery in a way—Thanksgiving in a prison camp. But we all have plenty to be thankful for. We are alive and well, and there are very many others who were with us not long ago, who are not.

Mostly, our celebration will assume the air of an orgy—of eating. An orgy purchased at the cost of weeks of skimping on food and fuel. But skimping like that is worth it in our eyes. Worth it, just once to have a hot breakfast, just once to have a hot—and adequate—lunch, worth it to have a really big supper. Worth it to have our fill, just once, of the sweets we crave.

And so we'll have it—and then start skimping again for Christmas, even though we hope we won't spend that holiday here.

Probably all be sick—but it's even worth that.

Some good news, too—a shipment of shoes, underclothing and good G.I. army blankets has arrived from the Red Cross and will be distributed soon. The blankets will be most welcome, since the two German Army blankets we have are "ersatz" and damned poor protection against this penetrating cold. Makes it rough when, in addition to the hardness of your bed, you can't sleep for the cold.

Weather has been unaccountably clear for three days now, and the almost windless days have brought bitter cold and heavy frost—ground hardening like rock underfoot.

Which makes it grand for walking, but uncomfortable for most other pursuits, such as washing and going to the toilet. But a more important result may be forthcoming, we hope. That would be improving fighting conditions on the fronts.

Chapter 7

♦

December, 1944

December 1, 1944
Sagan

The day after Thanksgiving, for the sake of my own amusement later, and whatever posterity may struggle through these notes some day.

For it was an occasion, and no mistake. Results were the same, almost, as if we'd had a prolonged drinking bout. We are all groggy right now.

We stuffed ourselves day-long with coffee, and bread and the sweets we crave so much—all made up into the most wonderful and fearful assortment of dishes ever conceived or eaten by so-called civilized man.

I know that at a distance it will seem supreme foolishness to save food for weeks, only to blow it in one day. But it was an unimaginable pleasure, just for once, to get up from the table fully satisfied.

Today, again, we are poor people, back on our iron rations. And before I forget it, here was our menu yesterday:

Breakfast: oatmeal, two slices of bread (toasted), coffee, fruit cake with chocolate icing. Lunch: baked potatoes with cheese sauce, carrot and cabbage salad, two slices of toast, coffee, fruit cake with icing. Brew (at 4 P.M.): coffee, graham crackers with chocolate icing. Dinner: chili corn carne (from personal parcels), mashed potatoes in large quantity, dried peas, baked Spam with cheese, two slices of bread, apricot pie. Brew (at 10 P.M.) coffee, fruit cake with chocolate icing.

I'll admit it was almost a shameful stuffing, but we did it shamelessly enough. Our diversions have been few enough, Lord knows.

Morale went up 100 percent.

One result—though one not generally discussed in polite society—was immediate and emphatic bowel-movements.

For us, this is a serious matter in many ways. For one thing, our toilets are outhouses, smell mightily, and are unconscionably cold. For another, we have only one supply of paper, and that from the Red Cross shipments. The Germans put out no paper. Any serious depletions in the paper by such an unexpected "run" is of necessity a problem.

The Wrong Side of the Fence

Still no mail from home. Makes it increasingly hard to write letters—so little I can say, anyway, and nothing to answer.

December 7, 1944
Sagan

Third anniversary of Pearl Harbor. When that attack came, I was sitting quietly at home. Now I'm sitting quietly too, though of course (see dateline) not home.

The date finds me in a somewhat depressed mood—a combination of a small setback in the news, lack of any information from home, scanty food, and being still a prisoner, I guess.

Certainly the news is not really bad. The drive on the West front has continued all week—though at a maddeningly slow pace in terms of our maps, and the Russians have opened up and are making splendid gains in Southwestern Hungary, having already reached Lake Baloton, and launching new attacks around Budapest.

But—and on such a slim thread is my reasoning hung—the attack on the West has not broken through, at least not yet, and two days ago OKW said the attacks around Aachen had slackened "due to high losses". This statement seems to be borne out by later news, although whether it is temporary or not is not yet apparent. As I've said before, it is inconceivable to me—to most of us—that such an attack should have been launched without sufficient preparation to permit it to carry through. I know this, and think I believe it'd been done, and yet—doubt creeps in now. Understand, I am no military strategist, and am certainly not in possession of enough facts to criticize the decisions now being made. But doping out the progress of the war has become an obsession.

Had a play again this week—"Night Must Fall"—and the boys did a masterful job of handling a tough dramatic problem.

Weather has been remarkable, reasonably dry, though cold. So we get in our quota of walking.

December 10, 1944
Sagan

Another three days gone, and as yet no great developments on the West. OKW yesterday admitted the loss of Julich on the Roer, and said today that Allied preparations in that sector indicated that another attack would be forthcoming. Meanwhile, the Italian front has come to life around Faenza, and the Russ make good progress towards Austria.

Continuing my program of self-education—however haphazard it may seem—I've been reading biographies. Currently, Van Doren's "Benjamin Franklin". Will do some reading on Rousseau next—prompted by a recent reference to his teachings (in print) which made it immediately apparent that I know almost nothing about him.

December, 1944

Of late, I am constantly surprised—and something ashamed, too—by the number of such references to famous authors or books or events that I have come upon and passed by, simply because the context has appeared to explain the reference satisfactorily. Thus I've been kidding myself for years that I knew a great many things well that I really only know in passing, as it were.

For example, I remembered of Franklin that he edited "Poor Richard's Almanac", got lightning from a cloud with a kite, was a signer of the Declaration of Independence—and that's almost all. I had no idea at all of the man's tremendous mental versatility, nor of his many and real contributions to his country and to science.

In the same view—determination to improve my enforced stay by widening my mental horizon—I've procured from the chaplain a copy of the Bible, and have set myself to read it from end to end—as a story and a history. I'm not deeply religious, but here again is a book that I profess to others to know, which I hardly know at all—excepting for some trite phrases I learned in childhood.

And so, between the reading, the necessary work of the combine (such as KP once a week), the work of keeping myself and my clothing clean (I washed and darned a sock tonight, for example), helping Delaney with his newspaper, walking the perimeter whenever possible, and attending classes (lately Meteorology), I manage to fill in the otherwise meaningless days here.

Despite the approach of Christmas, our food situation has not eased, there being but eight weeks supply (at our present half-rations) now in storage here. Germans seem determined not to permit us to keep any excessive supplies on hand.

No mail from home yet for any of us—and we all try to be philosophical as may be about it, though we all expect it now momentarily. Have had no sign of what has become of Dave. Wonder if he might even have been re-patriated? Probably impossible.

But, lack of mail notwithstanding, my thoughts turn homeward always, thinking of pleasant things in the past, planning pleasanter ones for the future. Absence does make the heart grow fonder—I feel myself closer to Ann now than ever before. And determined to make up to her something of the past two drab, worrisome years.

Random thought: This gang is certainly going to be law-abiding when it gets out of the Army. After this experience, none of us, I think, would ever do anything to put himself in danger of imprisonment again.

December 13, 1944
Sagan

Yesterday we had ice-cream, a treat I never expected to enjoy as a POW. Ice we obtained from puddles of water, our freezer was, as usual, made of tin cans, and the ingredients included powdered milk, flour, a "D" bar, sugar, crackers. We pronounced the result perfect.

The Wrong Side of the Fence

Since eating is the high spot of our day, we count no effort too much to work a change in our diet. Hence the ice-cream, plus numerous wondrous dishes we have improvised.

On eating, by the way, the Germans have told us they will try to get us beer for Christmas—the current spiritless variety, but beer, nevertheless. Since, some time ago, men attempted to escape from the camp in beer-kegs, we haven't had any here—none in my time, anyway.

Germans will charge us the outrageous price of 2 and a half marks per glass—about $1.10 at their valuation—for it. But the money comes out of the $28 per month they are supposedly paying me which I never see, so it makes very little difference what the price is.

And I'd like some beer.

December 17, 1944
Sagan

I've joined a mustache derby. I know it's foolishness, but I've always wanted to try one, and never had the courage to go through the initial stage in public. But here the public is uncritical, and it's a good chance to see what I can do in the way of lip-foliage. It comes off, though, at the first hint of going home.

Post has been manfully struggling to raise a mustache for some months now, and has finally succeeded in raising enough to be visible to the naked eye. He claims he's going home with it, too.

Noted some time ago that the English-language publications we see here have changed their tone from one of invincibility to dire foreboding on the fate of Europe should Germany be defeated. Should also note the change in the German-language press (which I read in translation). It, too, has ceased to promise victory, but now talks of honor, attempts to maintain morale by seizing on anything and everything that indicates any good German showing anywhere, pointing to the "Facts" that the Allies have been "forced" into a winter campaign and have made no great progress with it, harps on the Soviet influence, mentions mismanagement and starvation in the liberated countries. One said in a recent article that the situation now facing Germany is "worse than 1939."

A pretty good job of reversal.

Christmas now being one week away, our plans are pretty well formulated. There'll be a pageant based on the story of the three wise men, religious services, and the Germans have agreed to permit us to be out until 2 A.M. Christmas morning. Main observance, of course, will be eating well and fully again. And the fervent hope that we haven't much longer to wait.

The approach of this holiday season, by the way, has found me in an increasingly saddened mood. Thoughts of other holidays in other circumstances—freedom!—and again the slowness of the war, which makes it seem as if the day of deliverance from here is receding further and further into the future. It may not be so—we hope it won't be so—but the fighting on the West seems to be degenerating into the trench warfare of 1917, and that will make it even slower.

Been sleeping fully dressed (all but my shoes, of course), the past three nights, in an attempt to keep warm enough to sleep. Some of those G.I. blankets I spoke of before have been distributed, but I didn't get one, nor did Post. So for us these cold nights have been no pleasure.

Had a very light hard snow two days ago, which has now melted—and on the pines around the camp it makes a very pretty scene, one that I might have enjoyed at Christmas elsewhere. But cold. Cold.

For some days now we've been hearing the sounds of bombing and even of gunfire all around us. Must be within 50 or 60 miles, but no closer, since we haven't had any real air-raid alarms.

December 20, 1944
Sagan

A good day for me—very good. Excellent.

Got my first mail from home, direct. Three letters—one from Ann, one from Mother, one from Rev. Hartley (and if he knew I was seriously reading the Bible!).

The very sight of Ann's round, firm, rather childish hand, and Mother's printing, has brought a good deal to me—almost as if I heard their voices. Ann's note comes from Nebraska though it may well be that she has moved East again for the holidays, and it's good to hear from her that she's gaining a bit of weight—as if that could mean anything but good to me! And they both say they've been keeping in touch with the families of other members of the crew—so that's well. I've answered them at once.

But these letters, while they bring home so close to me, have proportionally increased my homesickness. Nothing to do about it, of course, but try to increase my capacity for patience. . . .

To add to the pleasures of today—and make it seem more Christmas-like, I was finally issued a new pair of shoes (a half-size too small, but brand-new Army brogans) and two pair of wool socks. And in the same mail as mine came notification to Kelly, from his wife, that he's been promoted to first lieutenant.

Just like Christmas, indeed.

Peculiar happenings on the West, with the Germans claiming that they have opened a full-scale offensive in the area near Luxembourg, as of Dec. 16—although as of today, they have claimed no gains for it and have been very indefinite about it, except to say that in four days they have captured 10,000 prisoners.

If true, that's a lot of prisoners, but at least until I can get conclusive evidence to the contrary, I take the attack as a very good sign for us. Reason that only really desperate conditions in their own lines (plus the need to provide the home front with some encouragement) would force them to an attack they cannot hope will meet more than a possible initial success, and which automatically increases the odds against them in the matter of loss of manpower. Either this, or they have decided to go out in a blaze of glory, rather than behind their defense lines.

I find, though, that the camp as a whole is much depressed by the news—emotions going up and down, as always, mercurially. We'll see.

Three men to the hospital last week, suffering "nervous breakdowns"—actually first signs of insanity. Surprising, in a way, how few of these cases there have been—six in all, in the past year and a half.

My reading program progresses. I've almost finished the Old Testament; have finished "Franklin", "Jeb Stuart"; "Paul Revere", a biography of Jacob Riis, and am now well into Arthur Train's "From the District Attorney's Office". Also, "The Gay Gaillard"—on Mary Queen of Scots.

A pretty catholic collection, but interesting.

December 23, 1944
Sagan

A gala week for me—I've received nine letters in the last three days (including one from the office and the one from Rev. Hartley) bringing me up to the end of October on the doings of Ann and the rest of the family, setting my heart at rest on the knowledge that they are well, but awakening me to added unrest in my desire to see them. Give me something to look forward to, too, in that both Ann and Mother mention the sending of tobacco and another parcel.

I'm somewhat chagrined that Post and Cole have thus far not received any mail—but try to fill them in with whatever concerns them or the crew as a whole from my mail.

Adding to the spirit of the season, the YMCA has shipped some crepe paper, with which we are decorating the barracks; our canteen has received and issued numbers of razors, brushes, combs, shaving soap, etc.; and we have been issued Christmas Red Cross parcels containing pipes, games, canned turkey, plum pudding, candy, etc. In all, considering the circumstances, it could be a great deal worse.

Weather continues fiercely cold—so cold the pool in the center of the compound has an eight-inch ice coating on it, and we are attempting to make an ice-skating rink.

And sleeping for me is almost impossible. Have learned something, though—if I cover my head with the blankets, my breath will act as a sort of automatic heater under the covers for a while—until I fall asleep. Then, of course, I get cold again and wake up.

Skies are clear at night, and unbelievably beautiful with stars.

Can't reach any conclusion on the news as yet—whether it's serious, expected, unimportant or what.

Germans have made large claims of battle and prisoners taken, but are curiously reticent about defining the limits of their drive, and objectives. Still,

December, 1944

they do claim to have driven a wedge some 24 miles deep, to be forcing Allied withdrawals from Aachen and Saar positions, though they say there is "heavy fighting" in the Saar.

Only estimate I can make at the moment: If the German attack was in any way anticipated by the Allies, it will shorten the war considerably. If not—if it shows as a real Allied blunder—it may delay conclusion a couple of months at most. Not very profound, but the best I can do at the moment.

By the way, the mustache is off. Got to be too annoying, and didn't like the looks, anyway.

December 26, 1944
Sagan

The day after Christmas—and depression again.

Not that we didn't have a good time. Or as good as we have any right to expect here.

We ate heavily but more sensibly, I believe, than on Thanksgiving, and so had fewer cases of stomach distress, though the usual run on the toilets. And since we were on parole, we were not locked into the barracks until 2 A.M., and had not Appels all day.

And the weather, again, was beautifully clear, though cold, and we could get exercise. And the food was excellent—turkey (canned, but the first some of us have tasted in two or three years), and candy and canned plum pudding; and the Germans even contributed by giving us some hats of paper and cheap noisemakers.

And we had religious services, and our band played jive and sweet in the various barracks during the day and night.

All of which seems to add into a pretty complete, full day—and we tried to make it so. But for most of us, it was palpably an empty show. You knew that beneath it all our thoughts were elsewhere, with other companions on other Christmases. There are many men here who have spent two such occasions right here.

Don't believe it's the religious aspects, but rather the sentimental, that affect.

Getting off the subject a bit (though I should also mention that the German radio also carried Christmas programs). I received a diploma today from Col. Spivey, for my work in the Sociology class.

It means little to me except as a souvenir, since I took this course and am taking others for my own edification. But similar certificates, attesting study under the most difficult circumstances, will mean a great deal to the many men who will try to continue their education after the war.

We're still in a quandary over evaluating the news.

OKW indicates the Germans have penetrated at some points as much as 40 miles behind our lines, yet its claims have been so nebulous as to gains that

The Wrong Side of the Fence

it is hard to see their objective. Though I believe it is becoming apparent that whatever the objective, they have not obtained it.

Unless it is, as we suspected, a diversionary move. Or it maybe a last gasp.

In any case, weather on the front has cleared, and our air force is now out in force, and heavy counter action is under way, OKW says.

Wrote again to Mother, and Boughton at the office, yesterday—will write also to Ann tonight. And pray, as always, I can see her soon.

During the holidays, by the way, the German troops living in the barracks across the fence from ours have had their families visiting them. Among these families there is quite a gang of good-looking youngsters aged anywhere from two to eight years. These kids have been playing cheerfully and unconcernedly behind the barbed wire all day—and the sound of their voices at games in such a place is strange indeed.

December 28, 1944
Sagan

The news takes a turn for the better again, with OKW indicating that the German drive on the West is virtually stopped, and "pitched", "Very heavy", "violent" fighting going on—under constant Allied air attack (which they seem to consider unfair) on all sides of their salient.

It begins to appear that they hoped to force the withdrawal or collapse of our West-front attack—and that they have failed to do so. And I begin to believe they may have gambled very near their all on the success of the movement—and, having lost, may lose the whole business rapidly now if we can bring up enough offensive power quickly.

Meanwhile, the Russ take giant strides in Hungary, almost completely surrounding Budapest, and going forward to the North and West. Good show.

After more than a week of bitter cold, the weather has eased this afternoon, and a light snow is falling.

◆ ◆ ◆

But better than the slight rise in temperature was the arrival of more G.I. blankets—one of which I got. So my sleeping problem is eased, I think.

For the benefit of future laughter, my nighttime sleeping arrangements go like this:

First, me dressed in long underwear, socks, pants and shirt; next, G.I. blanket (doubled over for extra warmth); next, German army blanket, single, tucked in deeply on all sides; next my quilt, made of doubled-over German blanket stuffed with newspaper; next, my overcoat and all other clothing I have.

Most of us sleep in similar fashion—I think because we don't eat enough to generate body-heat sufficient to keep us warm all night. Certainly the difference in body-heat is immediately noticeable after such meals as we ate Christmas and Thanksgiving.

December, 1944

Our ice-rink, built at the cost of much hard labor carrying jugs of water in the sub-zero cold, was opened day before yesterday and proved a surprising success. Skates, (strap-ons) are provided by the YMCA.

However, I managed to strain (I think) a tendon somehow at the back of my right leg—so making even walking an annoyance, let alone skating. And to add to my physical ills, I broke several fillings out of a tooth yesterday, and must now wait my turn to see the camp's one dentist (an English prisoner). Hope he can at least put cement in, until I can get proper dental treatment again.

By the way, one of the boys in Barracks 43 picked up the perfect bridge hand the other night—13 diamonds. He passed at first (thinking it a mistake), but was rescued by his partner and eventually reached seven diamonds, doubled and redoubled.

Chapter 8

♦

January, 1945

January 1, 1945
Sagan

Pardon the special marking on this entry—but a man has to mark the start of a brand new year somehow. Our own celebration was markedly quiet—as compared to others—and there was of course no carousing.

But for us, as for many others, this is truly a year of hope.

Snowed heavily all day yesterday, and picked up a good five inches by nightfall, making our surrounding pine trees, barbed wire, sentry boxes and drab barracks look faintly like something on a picture-post-card "winter" scene.

The snow brought a welcome rise in temperature, and (to part completely from pretty pictures) I took advantage of the break in the weather to do some much-needed laundry.

New Year's celebration consisted of a good breakfast and our usual lunch and supper, and then staying up until 2 A.M., wishing each other the best, and making some very mild noise at midnight.

Today we had no Appel—being on parole again, as at Christmas—and so slept late. The heavy snow cut out walking possibilities, and so—except for a few ice-skating enthusiasts—we held down activities to chess and card playing. But tonight we had the band in the barracks (it has been visiting each barracks in turn this past week) and put on an impromptu show for ourselves which we hugely enjoyed.

Occurs to me I may have been painting an unnecessarily grim picture in these notes. But we have not lost our American gift of humor—and there is real talent here. So we are able to make each other laugh, to amuse ourselves, to forget, for a while, where we are.

News has definitely turned to the better—the German drive is stopped and going backwards, OKW has been making excuses for days. I feel optimistic—if we can only catch 'em right, it may shorten this business very greatly.

Starting another class this week—English grammar.

And my reading course continues. Have finished the Bible, and am now going back to re-read sections I didn't grasp too well. And have finished

H. McNair Wilson's "Napoleon—the Portrait of a King", and "Daniel Boone" by Bakeslee.

Education—belated, but education nonetheless.

January 5, 1945
Sagan

Post got his first mail from home (his wife) yesterday, and two more letters today, and Cole also got a letter from his family today—and we are all in some kind of touch with home again. I'm very glad, since I've felt a little guilty about my own mail luck—though I've had no mail since Christmas.

I'm cook for the combine (with George) this week—thus going back on my prediction that I'd never cook here.

Reason is that Applegate, after four months of service, resigned as permanent cook the other day, although George, who has been his assistant, stayed on. Don't blame Applegate, it's a tedious and mostly thankless job. The cook is of necessity the custodian of all supplies, and sometimes our arguments over what's being done with those supplies get nastier than they should—all on the cook's head, too.

So to my other accomplishments, add that of cook—of sorts. Can't hurt me, and I'll have a better appreciation of home problems. Problem is, with George's help, not to hurt anyone else.

Speaking of my cooking stint, this place has proved a startling exposition of how much time humanity must needs devote to the business of living—to the supplying of even the most elementary wants.

Granted that we have little else to do here, still we are under the necessity of working almost entirely without the tools such work ordinarily demands, and must improvise even pots and pans and plates to eat from, before proceeding to the matter of cooking.

Even with the basic tools made or provided, four of the twelve of us devote ourselves entirely to cooking every day (two cooks, two KPs), while all the others are on constant call to aid in carrying bulk foods, fuel, etc.

All of us spend at least a day a week doing laundry, mending and sundry similar jobs.

And we spend considerable other time fixing and making our beds, attempts at bathing, shaving and washing (these last being major problems because of need to heat water). Added to these are the remainder of our activities—which consist of doing what we can to keep mentally and physically fit.

Coming from a civilization that provided or made easy most of these things and that in addition kept hidden the very processes that made them possible, this has proved a revelation to many of us. We begin to see that, however masked, the essential business of life is to prolong life by providing the wherewithal.

These are new thoughts to me.

The Wrong Side of the Fence

Have been reading the text of Hitler's and Goebbels' New Year's speeches. Without trying to read any special significance into them, they sound about as one would normally expect—encouragement, rather frank summations of the war situation, a note of hope. These people are certainly surprising in their conduct of the war to date—though it is obvious that they are hanging on now for better peace terms, since they know they cannot obtain victory.

Excitement last night—two of the boys made a successful escape through the fence. Guards in the compound searching all night—secret well kept, they haven't found out who escaped as yet. Better not to make any further mention here—never know who may read.

January 11, 1945
Sagan

After snowing heavily (about three inches) last night, it has been raining intermittently all day. As usual, it's a hardship on us, though a blessing in that we can sleep warm.

As always, the weather makes things depressing, so we busy ourselves at whatever comes to hand—I with some additional laundry, Kramer with tutoring French, Cole and Applegate with their jobs as rations officers, the others studying, doing tinwork, and other small projects.

Incidentally, I believe this is the reason that we twelve in this combine have been able to get on with so little friction—not always the case in camp. Each of us pursues some interest, we keep busy and out of each others' way as much as possible. Thus, Bascom is an assistant librarian and studies agriculture in odd time; George is cooking permanently; I work with Delaney and do a bit of studying and news analysis; Post studies avidly, as does Eatinger; Cole and Applegate do rations work for the barracks, etc.

The news swings upwards for us. Yesterday, plotting OKW admissions on our maps, we found that the Allies have narrowed the neck of the German penetration to about seven miles at Bastogne, and today OKW admitted a retreat (and called it that) back from St. Hubert across the Ourthe. And the Russ keep going towards Austria, by-passing Budapest.

Col. Spivey spent an evening in the barracks two nights ago, explaining things in general, trying to give us straight dope on many subjects having to do with our relations with the Germans, drawing on his knowledge of the Army to answer what he could of our many questions.

Also, two days ago, I finally got to the dentist, who did an excellent and quick job in fixing my filling-less molar. A Britisher, he was cheerful and clean, working with excellent German-made drills, but with only temporary material for fillings. Hope it holds up until I can get better attention.

January 13, 1945
Sagan

Germans say the Russ have started a major offensive West of the Dneiper

And we seem to have stopped and turned back the German push on the East. Things heading up, looks like.

Add to my list of books read: Lytton Strachey's "Elizabeth and Essex"; Fast's "Citizen Tom Paine"; N. B. Baker's "Juarez"; a growing and most catholic collection.

◆◆◆

We've been having a discussion over bread—how to split up five slices per day per man so that each man gets as much out of it as possible. It illustrates some of our petty difficulties here, and provides a startling parallel to small arguments that get started at home.

For some time now, in order to make our scant food supplies go 'round, we have rationed ourselves to five slices of bread—and to save butter and jam (this last important because we have no other sweetening) the man doing KP has been doing all the buttering and spread all the jam.

But the system has caused friction, because we get hungry at odd times. And, since bread is the only "extra" food we have, we've taken to "borrowing" —eating tomorrow's bread tonight, which has resulted in real confusion over just who has how many slices due him or owing to the combine. Plus the fact that I would rather have two slices in the morning, none at noon and two at supper, than spreading them out one slice to a meal; while Post would like one at breakfast, none at noon, three at night, etc.

Remedy proposed was to issue each man his five slices in the morning, let him do as he pleased with it through the day. So the twelve of us sat down to discussion quite solemnly.

Giving out the bread would also mean rationing out jam and butter. If we started that, where would it stop? How about cheese? Or meat, for that matter?

It took considerable restraint for us—grown men, remember—to keep the argument from getting vicious, as we argued the pros and cons.

Final result: We each get our five slices, and a modicum of jam, each day.

The shaving of heads in the—to me—vain hope of thus insuring return of abundant locks to heretofore thinning polls, has come into fashion again. There are five such shining skulls in the barracks now. Can't see the sense in it myself, but it is an occasion for comment, and indubitably something to do.

Up to the time I came here, searchlights in the night never meant anything but friendliness—the home airport, or a beacon to mark the way. But one more picture of Stalag III I'll always carry with me is night here—with powerful lights on every sentry box, incessantly sweeping the grounds, the fences, the barracks, picking a man up the moment he leaves a building at night, following him relentlessly. Reminder always that we are watched.

The Wrong Side of the Fence

January 14, 1945
Sagan

A brief note to spot the news: In one day, the Russ have advanced about 25 miles towards Krakow and opened a new front in East Prussia. And the Allies are on the offensive along a good part of the West front.

Maybe <u>this</u> is it—maybe I haven't far to go into the sixth notebook of these scribblings, after all!!

◆ ◆ ◆

This is the sixth book of these notes, and I feel an autobiographer when I look backward over my notes—already ready to edit, to delete and add here and there, to put the best light on things. But on second thought, I don't think it should be changed. I believe these notes are a rather accurate measure of my thoughts and hopes and feelings—and those of a good many of my fellows.

And I open this book with plenty of hope that it won't take too much more writing to finish the story.

Our friends, the Russ, have been going at a tremendous rate since they opened up almost simultaneously all along the East front January 12. By tonight, according to OKW, they were already astride the German border West of Kielce and at a point north of there; have already by-passed Warsaw; are advancing in East Prussia and in Czechoslovakia—in fact, as of tonight, they are only 70 miles from Breslau, thus, at the closest point, only 160 miles from Sagan. This is immense—a pace of something like 25 miles a day.

What remains to be seen is how much—if any—a barrier the Germans' vaunted Eastwall will offer.

We are somewhat dubious about news from the West—all of us looking to see something in the nature of a major drive there. This may have been thrown out of kilter by the recent, ill-fated German attack, but on second thought we may have seen the beginning of it in the recent heavier attacks at Malmedy and Vielsalm and East of Bastogne. In any event, the Allies are on the move, attacking everywhere again, driving them back.

And, of course, the advance from the East brings up the perennial question of how it will end for us—whether we'll be moved out or not as the Germans attempt to hang onto us as hostage, what will be done with us when we reach our own Army again, the possibilities of trouble with the civilian population hereabouts, etc.

Anyhow, with the news good, our spirits go up and up—the clusters around the newsroom maps grow larger, speculation is rife—most of us try, half-heartedly, to hang onto our hopes, to deny to ourselves and each other that there's a possibility of a quick ending—afraid of another disappointment that might be hard to take. But in our hearts we can't keep away from the thought—this might very well be the final drive.

It may seem, like Shakespeare's characters in "Julius Caesar" that we protest too much, for having done relatively so little ourselves—or should I say, myself.

January, 1945

But that argument I refute with all my soul. We are young—and this is no place for a young man; we are all willing to pay the price—that we're here instead of six feet under is by God's own intervention in most cases; in a word, we would have done more, except for the fortunes of war.

At the order of the Lagerkommandant (the German camp commandant), we go on full parcels Monday for a two-week period. Germans are again getting excited over the knowledge that we have any food at all in reserve—they are afraid that with the Russ approach we may try a mass break, even provide reserve food for paratroops, or something. To us, it means more nearly adequate food.

After serving me faithfully for these many months, my watch broke today—somehow I managed to tear out the winding stem. A present from my old office, I've had that watch now nearly two years—all through my Army career, my flights, my jump, imprisonment.

Took it to Lt. Jerry Kethley—who used to run a jewelry store in his native Texas—and, with what materials he could find, he will try to fix it for me.

Odd how an inanimate piece of machinery like a watch can assume a personality. For instance—woke up the other night for some reason and couldn't get to sleep again. Got to feeling lonely and homesick and sorry for myself, staring into the darkness, and finally looked at my watch's luminous dial to see the time. The dial looked friendly, somehow, and the busy ticking of the works was very friendly and reassuring.

For the first time in more than a year, the Germans are allowing inter-compound visits between the four American camps here—these to take the form of inter-compound games. And in order to accommodate them, the whole camp (including our six colonels) worked feverishly in bitter cold weather today to build another skating rink of regulation size. Something to do, but no particular pleasure in the biting wind.

Odd thing happened two days ago. Our radio—over which we get OKW news and other German programs, suddenly blurted out a full broadcast of news in <u>English</u>, from BBC.

No explanation—the main receiving set is manipulated from the Vorlager by the Germans and "piped" in over wires to us. Probably carelessness, but sounded wonderful.

January 19, 1945
Sagan

The news keeps piling up! Russ going at a tremendous pace—Warsaw has fallen, Krakow has fallen, penetrations into East Prussia—Littsmanstadt (that used to be Lodz) which is 15 or 20 miles within the new German border, is now in Russ hands; the whole front moving at great speed. Witness: today a steady stream of German training planes, transports, and other aircraft, flying over our heads, all going West—away from the shifting lines.

The Wrong Side of the Fence

No action on the West as yet—though we look for it day-to-day now. Russ air-raid on Breslau last night—we could see the flashes in the Eastern sky.

Optimism is high, decisions are being made right now, we feel.

The unexpected gift of 1000 British Christmas parcels that arrived recently—plus the prospect of full parcels next week—has gone far towards boosting morale and well-being. Combination of food and news is almost too much, but pleasant, nevertheless. Hope it isn't the proverbial fattening of the calf, though.

Today was a red-letter day in another way, too—I finally got a pair of shoes to wear. Ordinary, unlovely Army brogans they are—and a bit too small and too wide—but I can and am wearing 'em, praise be. Was almost barefoot before this. Better fixed for a possible move out of here on foot now. Cut down my old shoes for slippers.

Camp did a generous thing tonight. We were told that at a camp some two miles from here, some 3000 Allied prisoners taken at Arnheim desperately needed supplies. So from our own meagre possessions—because we know the worth—we sent some 1500 packs of cigarettes, underwear, pants, shirts, jackets, blouses, and related items.

The poor help the poor.

January 21, 1945
Sagan

Wish I could communicate to paper the tremendous tension that hangs over the camp like a pall tonight—gripping everyone's nerves and making them taunt as bow strings (if I may mix metaphors a bit).

The tension has been mounting steadily as the moment of decision—and the Russ—draw closer and closer.

Accentuated for us by the continuing exodus of all types of planes to the West—we have watched gliders, observation planes, all types of training ships, the big awkward lumbering JU 52's, many others, going Westward over us to the interior.

The moving of all of us (some 40,000 prisoners in this area) from this area is now a very distinct possibility. Under the Geneva Convention, the Germans are bound to move POW's out "of the immediate area of fighting" as soon as possible. And, of course, it would be extremely foolish to think they would abandon valuable hostages to an advancing army.

However, the only transportation available for such a mass exodus that we can see at present would be our own feet. And the prospect of walking possibly several hundred miles through hostile country in the dead of winter, poorly dressed and shod and fed as we are, is not a pleasant one. And we may be lucky at that—we hear that such marches are already under way from the camps further East.

In any event, our camp command has wisely taken such action as it can for the eventuality, shuffling and re-shuffling clothing, shoes, and other necessi-

January, 1945

ties to insure wherever possible that everyone has at least a minimum of needed items should the need arise. And since that need may come at any time, we keep our few necessities at hand at all times.

The tension builds up and up—an unhealthy thing, but one we can't help of course.

"Volkisher Beobachter", the Nazi Party organ, Thursday carried a lengthy report in very frank language stressing the gravity of the situation in the East, calling on the people to stand fast and hold faith, explaining that the German High Command hopes to withdraw to another line—the "Eastwall"—and there stem the Russian drive. But the Red Army keeps coming at a pace almost terrifying even to us, seemingly brushing aside its own losses and opposing troops with equal disregard. On the West, the Allies seem to hold the initiative again, but for the moment are doing little.

Meantime, there is no other important topic of conversation among us— even plans for the future being held in abeyance, now that we must wait so breathlessly for what the unforeseen, but very immediate future, holds for us. Worst of it is, as usual, that we ourselves have no semblance of control over what happens now.

And we watch that stream of planes flying over us constantly—Westward.

January 23, 1945
Sagan

The tension goes on, but we have quieted to watching now, after the past two days of activity. Our future is still uncertain enough. The Russ today, according to OKW, are nearing Posen—only 85 miles Northeast of us, and are within 10 miles of Breslau—80 miles away on that side. And they have almost cut East Prussia in half.

And today, we know we are in a battle zone—or every close to it. For, knifing through the continuing stream of transport aircraft that flee West, came seven or eight flights of German fighters—heading East. They carried bombs as they went overhead—and returned empty in a few minutes. More air activity than anyone has seen here in two years.

So the move may come at any time, but we feel better about it, having put ourselves in the best order we can.

Most of us spent the last two days in sewing and mending our few clothes, making sure each man had a minimum of socks, etc., contriving all manner of strange devices to serve as knapsacks and carry-alls, putting our things where we can reach them quickly.

Of necessity, most of us have become pretty fair rough and ready tailors— and we put our talents to work. I find I can darn a sock with the best, and found plenty of work in that direction and in the construction of a pair of mittens out of an old towel, an old shirt and a pair of badly-worn woolen gloves—an example emulated by Hamilton and Webb, among others. Out of the remains of the same towel, I manufactured a pair of straps with which to sling my canvas

The Wrong Side of the Fence

dufflebag (that I was issued back at Wetzlar) over my shoulders. Cole, considerably more ingenious and painstaking, succeeded in cutting and sewing a similar bag into a very creditable knapsack. Post and Applegate made musette-type bags. Kelly converted an old shirt into a knapsack by sewing up the bottom and front, using the sleeves as straps. Some of the others plan to carry blanket-rolls.

And this was repeated ad infinitum around the camp.

◆ ◆ ◆

Went ice-skating today for the first time in nearly ten years—and did quite creditably. Like swimming, I imagine it's something you don't forget easily. And the ice on our two rinks is excellent. Post went with me—and though he has never skated much, did better than I. He didn't flop—but I did, a beautiful header caused by a big hole.

Our general and two colonels also skating—and pretty well, too—so I was in good company all 'round.

Weather has been bitterly cold again—24 below zero centigrade this morning, and as always, a real problem to get warm and stay that way.

Added to this is the ever-present food problem. Though we are on full parcels, we are trying to save out chocolates, cheese, and such items against the possibility of a march. And on top of that, we had no bread ration for three days—Germans saying they are having transportation difficulties, which we can believe. Yesterday, too, the Germans took away some hundreds of loaves of bread we had in storage—to feed refugees, they said.

And today they are digging up some of the potatoes they stored shortly ago, also to feed refugees, we are told.

January 27, 1945
Sagan

Tension has definitely eased in the last three days. Most of us have reached the inescapable conviction that we <u>will</u> be moving shortly, either with the Germans or the Russ.

I do not believe the Germans will attempt to move us now, while the pressure on them is so great and while their own transportation situation is complicated by the problem of refugees and troop movements, but it is certain that should the Russ be stopped somewhere on the Oder (where they are now), they will move us out.

To move us by railroad right now, though, would be impossible, we think. They couldn't possibly assemble enough cars to move all of us.

The Russ are moving, though, and fast. As of tonight they are at Stienau—only 40 miles to the East, and we can occasionally hear the rumble of the guns. We can measure the approach of the battle by another sign too—the furious, and I might say, frantic air-activity we see.

All day, every day for the past four days, every conceivable German fighting plane—Stukas, HI 111's, Junkers, FW 190, ME 109—that can fly has swept

January, 1945

overhead, disappeared over our tree-shortened horizon for a short time, and then come streaking back to Westward.

And the railroad yard, just North of us, has been almost inactive. Today there were a series of heavy explosions in the direction of Sagan itself, which we were told were caused by dynamiting the ice on the little River Bober to serve as a tank barrier.

Elsewhere, the Russ have brought their lines up to the Oder from Oppeln to Streinau, have chopped off East Prussia completely, are 135 miles from Berlin itself. There is now a possibility beyond my wildest imaginings—that we may be released from here before the war itself is over!

Can't understand the West front, though—although OKW said tonight that the Allies had made a breakthrough (no other details) North of Julich in the Aachen salient.

The mail brought good news to Cole, Post and myself—among Post's letters was one from Mrs. Frank Hart, mother of our tailgunner, whose name has not appeared here so far.

Hart was the only member of our crew who was not picked up immediately, back there in Holland, and since neither we nor the Germans seemed to know what had happened to him, I have not mentioned him here. However, his mother writes enough that we can assume Frank was in the hands of the Underground for a while, which would account for the long silence.

My own letter—from Mother—is full of cheer, tells of packages on the way. She says, however, she hasn't heard from me since July.

◆ ◆ ◆

Fashion notes: Col. Spivey, our C.O., is bald down the center and top of his head. Thus, when a trio of hopeful hair savers, noting losses on the forehead, trimmed the center sections of their pates, the style was immediately dubbed a "Col. Spivey". Several other "Col. Spiveys" have appeared, though not since the Russ advances.

Heavy snowfall again last night—about four inches—and cold again today.

Got my watch back today too—Kethley worked a miracle on improvisation to find a stem that will permit me to wind it.

Col. Martin came into the library, where I'm writing, is calling for attention.

9:00 P.M., January 27, 1945

IT'S COME! WE ARE ORDERED TO LINE UP AT 10:45 P.M. TO MARCH OUT. ANOTHER CONCLUSION WRONG . . . .

January 30, 1945
Burau, Germany

We've been on the march over two days now under the most miserable conditions I have yet seen—a march that since yesterday has assumed something of the proportions of a disorganized rout.

The Wrong Side of the Fence

Hard to figure what the Germans think they are accomplishing—we have only made some 38 kilometers total distance since we started, going in an aimless sort of way to the Southwestward.

The guards accompanying us seem to have no idea where we're going or why. We are fortunate in that we carried some Red Cross food with us when we left, since the Germans to date have made no attempt to feed us at all—and have made only half-hearted attempts to even provide hot water so that we can get some sort of heat into our stomachs.

What little else we've had has come from an amazingly friendly civilian population, foreign workers and the like. Accommodations for us have been heatless, lightless, lacking anything approaching elementary comforts. They seem to have been haphazardly chosen as opportunity offered. Seems to be no plan or anything on this march.

Too cold to hold the pencil. . . . . .

January 31, 1945
Muzkau, Germany

I give up on day-to-day details. Too difficult, too miserable, too cold and too tired. So will just fill in dates and places, enlarging later—if at all.

Anyway, we left Sagan finally at 7:30 A.M., January 28, almost seven months to the day since we were shot down. Stood around in the below-zero cold for over three hours before marching out. Accompanied by entire German garrison, dogs, machine guns lined up along the march mounted on horse-drawn wagons.

Eerie sight—barracks in North camp burning silently but with a great orange light against the dark pines, as we move by.

Miserable walking—17 kilometers in all—through heavy, slushy snow, and snowing heavily besides all day. No sanitary arrangements along the way, no German food, no water. Silent, deserted towns, or towns where refugees line the roads in horse and cattle-drawn carts, waiting to move out. Seems orderly enough withdrawal. Little kids peeking out, red-faced with the cold, from under huge piles of household goods, clothes, as the refugees' wagons rattle by us, or plod phlegmatically alongside.

People left in towns seem to be all foreign workers—mostly Poles. Very friendly. Give us water and food at every opportunity in spite of surliness of guards—give it for nothing or a few cigarettes.

Kids along the way beg for sweets—"shokoladey" it sounds like. We haven't much ourselves—but they are kids. We give it to them.

In evening arrived at Halbau, where we stood in the 24-below temperature (centigrade) for more than three hours, while the Germans frantically sought accommodations. Most fantastic thing in the war, probably. We wandered up and down the town streets at will, practically take the place over for a while. Must keep moving to keep from freezing.

January, 1945

Finally, they march us to a Lutheran Church—over 1200 men (including Gen. Vanaman and five colonels) jammed into tiny building for maybe 250. Five hundred or more slept in crypt under the church—damp, no heat. More in outhouse behind building.

Miserable. No heat. Impossible for most of us to even lie down. General, who is 51, walked with us like a trojan all day, looks rocky now. We make a place for him to sleep.

Some few German troops moving up towards the front during the day—many more coming back. They look disorganized and unhappy—beg us for cigarettes, food.

No toilet in church—with guard's permission, we use churchyard. Snowing heavily, bitter cold, strong wind drives snow into every nook of the building, cuts through clothing.

Left Halbau early morning of 29th. Same murderous cold wind blowing, snowing, road icy. Wind so cutting, I have to dig towel out of my pack, wrap my face in it—feel as if face cut by knives. German guards as bad off as we are—many are older men, struggling under huge packs. We don't feel sorry for them, though they complain bitterly of cold.

My feet seem to be freezing. We stop walking every half-hour or so—find I can fall into snow and go to sleep if I dare. But feet get icy when we stop—takes couple of minutes walking to thaw them out.

Through endless, monotonously same-looking pine forests, finally arriving at Burau (see previous note) desperately cold. Tiny hamlet, deserted. We go to an old estate of some kind, now a government farm. We've been following German Route 99, circling slowly Southwest.

Bedded down for the night in huge barn full of wheat straw. One toilet provided—snow outside, none other. No heat. No lights. No attempt to feed us—and we running out of food now, except by foreign workers who somehow get a little hot water to us.

Many of the boys have obtained sleds or improvised them, and drag their stuff on them. March assumes more of the appearance of the retreat from Moscow.

My feet swelled so, can hardly get my shoes on again. Too cold to attempt drying socks.

All day 30th at Burau, we trying to make best of desperate situation, sleeping four under a blanket for warmth. Finally, overrun German guards somewhat. Find a kettle, melt snow, make hot water for selves. Try to keep warm—impossible. Dirty, sticky, bearded.

Left Burau morning of 31st for longest march to date—28 kilometers today to this place (Muzkau) where we are bedded to our immense amazement in an old brick kiln, which is warm, has lights and water.

Marched all day through deep, loose, shifting snow—with ice underneath—very tiring, like walking through sand on a beach. Shoes soaking wet. Feet freezing up every time we stop. Must wear overcoat—makes me sweat while we walk, but freeze when we stop.

The Wrong Side of the Fence

We are stumbling along almost like blind men, up over hills endlessly. No semblance of organization in ranks as when we started. Straggle all over the road.

Refugees on the road again, rattling past us. Still no German attempt to feed us—our own supplies getting really low. Post and I had "D" bar apiece to eat all day—nothing else—but it carried us amazingly well. Kelly has lost heel of his shoe—almost cripples him in back of leg.

Spent whatever time we could trying to barter with civilians along road—offering cigarettes for food of any kind. Post and I get some onions, a piece of bread.

German guards plod miserably along, pay no apparent attention to us. But dogs patrol edges of column, machine guns still in evidence.

Again through endless forest, many little towns (including Friebus) to here. Get to this place after dark, stood around in street for two hours—feet freezing. German troops wandering around, try to beg coffee from us. Finally got to this factory.

Dead tired—so warm here. Must stop.

Chapter 9

◆

February, 1945

February 1, 1945
Muzkau

We're staying here today, which we don't mind at all, since it gives us additional time to rest up, dry ourselves, remake our packs, etc.

The place a hotbed of rumors—as usual with any place we are. Latest one is that we leave here tomorrow morning by train (probably box-cars) to an old AAF sergeant's camp near Munich. Gonna be a long trip, and probably an uncomfortable one, but we've made it so far—we'll make it through.

Germans issued first food to us last night—couple slices of bread.

Rumor goes now that, thanks to General's insistence, and the guards' fears that this crowd will get completely out of hand if we aren't fed, we are to get a hot meal and more bread tonight.

Meanwhile—having subsisted for three days of heavy work on what we carried with us from Sagan, and having no real assurance of anything, we have all gone very lightly on food today. For example, Post and I (working together) had one slice—or rather, one-half slice—of bread, and coffee for breakfast; one cup of bouillon (with an onion we bartered for yesterday), one half slice of bread, for lunch; and are planning the same meal for supper.

Took an inventory a while ago, found we had between us the following:

About a quarter-loaf of bread, six bouillon cubes, four or five spoonfuls of Nescafe, a half-pound of sugar, a half-block of cheese, a "D" bar, a box of raisins—and that's all. And we have no idea when, if ever, we'll get more food. The others are about in the same fix.

Hot meal or not, we plan to make up the remaining bread, cheese and margarine into sandwiches against the morrow. Much easier to make them here—you can cut the bread easier and thinner—than on the road in the cold.

This factory—a brickworks—is German-owned, but seems to be entirely operated by Polish workers. We've been trying all day to trade with them—but these miserable folks have so little food themselves that we haven't the heart, almost, to take anything from them. But American cigarettes, soap, sugar seem to have tremendous value in their eyes (as to German civilians also) and they are willing to trade almost anything they have for them.

The Wrong Side of the Fence

Factory is operating, despite us swarming all over it. Three stories high, we are bunked over the kilns—escape-holes of which we use for cooking. First really warm place we've been in for days. However—only one toilet, one water tap, one must stand in line for these necessities.

A small enough discomfort.

◆ ◆ ◆

More on the march, so far:

How clean and orderly the small German towns look—and how cheerless and cold. Plenty small children in every town. Highway along which we march—covering more than a mile in our long, straggling, nondescript column—getting littered like an American street with cans, paper, etc., as we move.

In Friebus, old men who seem to be 80 or more, carrying long ancient rifles, watch us solemnly. Little kids in uniform too—seems as if every male on Germany from 5 to 85 is in some kind of uniform, carries weapons. Wehrmacht uniforms very seedy—some of these soldiers try to beg from us, others follow edges of our column, scavenging. Group of Russian prisoners working on the road. They wave and we shout "tovarisch" at them—all either of us can do.

That scene in Halbau as we wandered at will up and down the main street, driven by need to keep warm. Standing an endless hour in the biting cold until we got into that church—and then the impossible search for a place to sit down.

English-speaking German refugee on the road—shouting to us we're all in the same boat. His horses lathered, steaming. Lack of anything but horse-drawn transport for civilians, very few Army trucks—and those producer-gas driven. General appearance of desolation.

Miserable dry snow—makes walking so hard.

Guards with us now include some of the "hund postens" we had back at Sagan—who used to walk the compound at night with their dogs after lockup. Dogs are really beautiful animals—German shepherds—and wonderfully trained. Up to now, anyway, they pay no attention to us, stalking along behind their masters.

February 2, 1945
Muzkau

Now 11 A.M. and we're still here—seems (so rumor has it) that we're to remain another night, then hike another 18 kilometers or so, and there get a train.

Which we don't very much believe, since it would take an immense train to carry us and the remnants of West camp that are here. And the whole thing adds to the general impression of disorganization and confusion on the part of the Germans.

February, 1945

Anyway, they did issue some more bread last night—no hot meal. Good thing not walking today—thaw and rain last night stripped almost all the snow off the surrounding fields, and roads are a mess of slush and mud.

Main thing we miss is news—haven't had anything authentic for nearly a week—though we hear the Russ are within 47 miles of Berlin, and the West Front has opened up a bit. But it's maddening, after our steady diet of news, to have nothing to chew on. We know it's nearly over, but where the end will find us is another matter.

February 8, 1945
Moosburg, Germany

Did I note that it would take an immense train to move us! Huh!

But it's been six days since I made a note back at Muzkau, and want to make up all I can before everything gets completely confused in my head.

Remained at the brick factory all day the second—most of us improving our time by shaving and washing up as best we could (our last shave to date) and on that night were issued some Red Cross rations at the rate of one parcel to four men.

You can never imagine the solemnity with which we gathered around the boxes, carefully counting out the coffee-powder by the spoonful, the prunes by the number in the box (52) carefully considering the relative food value of a can of meat pate as against two cans of salmon (which Post and I took, by the way—looking to the convenience of carrying the salmon), the proper division of "D" bars, sugar, etc. It was of course deadly serious—we had no idea how far we might have to go on it.

For the night, Gomez discovered a pile of straw mats in the building which apparently had been used as air-raid blinds on the windows. Despite the objections of the guards, some adroit shifting and dodging brought them upstairs—a distinct improvement over the brick floor as a sleeping place.

Left Muzkau at 8:15 A.M., February 3, destination as usual unknown, but our road now angling Northwestward, completing the third side of a big square we seem to have been making since we left Sagan.

A fair-sized town, Muzkau, we found—must have been a big tourist center in its day. Full of hotels and restaurants, all with the same forlorn, empty look. Little narrow winding streets, houses in many colors, like a picture book.

We see quite a few Hungarian soldiers on the street, and at one stop, near what seems to be a military hospital, I try to talk to them in what little of the language I can remember. But, outside of being eager for cigarettes, they seem pretty confused themselves as to what they're doing. The Germans pay no attention at all to them—act as if they're not worthy of attention.

And so, on out of town. The rain and thaw have done a good job, and the roads—excellently paved, but narrow as in England—are for the most part dry.

The Wrong Side of the Fence

Again the road winds through endless, carefully-tended pine forests—sombre dark green interspersed with small plowed fields and occasional small farmhouses and towns.

As usual, there is no provision for water and sanitary needs, but we take care of the one by the roadside and barter for the other with civilians who seem willing to trade their hopes for the future for a few cigarettes or a bit of soap.

At one place along the road, we come on a group of civilian men—old men and young boys—armed with picks and shovels and mattocks, working to dig trenches under direction of a uniformed soldier. All along the roadside are small one-man trenches—just big enough for one man and a machine gun.

During the long, weary afternoon we have a heavy air bombardment to the North of us—can see the condensation-trails in the sky high above. Goes on for a long time. Air raid alarms blowing in towns we pass through, but they make no attempt to conceal us or stop us. Just keep on straggling through. We surmise the attack is being made on Berlin—we must be about South of there now.

Continue to be refugees on the road—lack of motor transport remains remarkable to us. One horse-drawn wagon marked "Breslau"—long trip to here that way.

Finally at 3 P.M., after 20 long kilometers, we arrive at the hamlet of Graustein—a tiny place without even a village square. The Germans break us up in groups of 90 or so and billet us in the villagers' barns. And those barns are filthy—though the houses seem neat enough.

Mud in the yards inches deep, a large manure pile behind the barn (where the water pump is), no toilet except the manure pile.

But the farmer, who tells us (when the guards have gone outside the barn) that he was a POW in England in the last war, finds us a carbide lamp so we can get settled in the hay, and his wife gets a small stove going so that we can have hot water—not enough for washing, but at least so that we can make coffee.

And then we learn the value of the little things we carry from America. Using the German-speaking talents of Lt. Fred Gwinner, we find that a few cigarettes, a couple of cakes of soap, a half-can of coffee and a little dried milk (a spoonful or two), produces a peck of potatoes, a pound of real honey, civilian-type bread.

With these, and a contribution of odd bits of canned fish, and other food, we make up a big vat of hot soup in the water-heater, with Cole and Applegate acting as cooks.

As thus to bed in the straw and freezing cold.

Up early in the cold grey dawn (and I mean that) on the Fourth, for a 14-kilometer hike to Spremberg—a sizable military town, we're told—where we are again supposed to entrain.

The walk is through the same sort of country we've been traversing, though getting hillier now—and there's no use to repeat details.

February, 1945

At Spremberg—or rather the edge of town—we find a really big German Caserne, an armory or training school for tank corpsmen, now populated by horse-drawn wagons, dummy tanks, and some sort of Wehrmacht troops in training.

These troops are a nondescript group—all extremes of ages and sizes, and willing to trade the very ornaments of their uniforms—regimental insignia and the like—for a few cigarettes. We establish a standard price for German money: 1 cigarette for any coin, 2 cigarettes for paper money up to a 20-mark note.

The school itself is a big place, big yellow-brick barracks and barns, with big golden imperial eagles out in front of the main buildings.

We've turned into one of the barns (along with about 20 horses who don't like our company) and we're told we'll get a hot meal, be held a couple of hours, given a full Red Cross parcel per man, and put on a train. We wander about the encampment more or less freely—build small fires to get warm, and discover that remnants of West Camp and Bellaria camp (who arrived here before us) are still here.

Among them, by strange coincidence, I discovered Bob Greenquist, with whom I went through my entire Army career, and whom I last saw last May when he went to Italy while I went to England. He's been down here since early June, tells me Dave First is also down. Also found Charles Edison—also out of my class at San Marcos.

Here we suddenly lose our General, along with Col. Spivey, Col. Kennedy, Capt. George—who are suddenly ordered to Berlin by OKW, we are told. We don't know why, of course, but speculation is immediate and wild. We even hear a rumor that the Germans have put out peace feelers. Of course we have no news of any authenticity at all, and have no real idea as to how things stand, except that the Russ and the Allies are still on the move.

Finally, at 4 P.M. we get some hot barley, and then move out of the camp for another four kilometers through, first, a model apartment house district, a large park and a fairly extensive business district—all of it apparently untouched by bombing.

It's Sunday—we've been en route a week—and again the whole town (including a good many wounded soldiers) is out to see us go by. Again they're curious, not resentful.

On another street a troop of Hungarian cavalry moves—beautiful horses.

Walk through the town brought us to a freight station—and there was our "train". Forty boxcars!

Forty boxcars, all French "40 x 8"—about which I'd read, but on which I never thought to ride. Tiny things, little four-wheeled carts about a third the size of one of our own freight cars at home. And we were crowded, 55 men, our packs, and a guard, into each. At about midnight, after an issue of another parcel (one to four men) we left in a great rattle and bang and tooting of whistles.

That was the 4th. By the 5th—anniversary of my commissioning—we had only made 30 kilometers towards Nuremberg (our supposed destination) after an interminable night of shunting and banging and waiting on sidings.

The Wrong Side of the Fence

From the fourth until last night the picture is again for me a confused jumble of misery:

Of bitter cold, of a car so crowded it was impossible for all to sit down—let alone sleep—at one time; of filth and grime and no opportunity to wash at all four days on end; of almost no water to drink—and none of it either clean or hot; of doing one's "business" out the door of the moving car; of being trampled on as men tried to reach the door; of being so miserable and uncomfortable and dirty that I didn't care to eat (but Post manfully made sandwiches, despite hands black with grime); of men getting sick and vomiting from the car door, or inside on everyone else if they couldn't make the door; of Bob Moore getting taken in a fit the second day (at Zwikau) and taken off the train with pneumonia; always of biting cold, darkness, dirt—the tin cans we use as our only utensils getting filthier visibly.

Not much chance for sightseeing, our "side-door pullman" not being made for it—but the general impression the same. A sombre, dark, brooding countryside under leaden, forbidding skies.

Through Chemnitz, Stuttgart, Nuremberg, to Munich (all badly bombed from what we saw) we rattled, finally being shunted Northeastward from Munich to Moosburg, site of an old enlisted men's camp—big place, now populated by Russ, Poles, French, Indians, English. Here we are to be deloused—cleaned up (we hope) then sent elsewhere. We'll see. More later.

February 9, 1945 (Friday)
Moosburg

What a dump this is!

But maybe it looks worse to me because I'm sick and miserable (as are several hundred others), with a case of diarrhea that has weakened me considerably, but which beyond that is not apparently serious.

Nearly half of us were sick last night and today, and the scenes weren't pleasant. Boys unable to reach the door of this so-called barracks in time, vomiting and doing other things on everyone else. Sickness probably result of a combination of 13 days without hot food, nerves, dirt, filthy eating utensils, fatigue, and several other things, I imagine.

Particularly, drinking water obtained from farmyards (because there was no other provision of water for us), where the pumps stood in the middle of a manure pile or in other general filth.

Add memories of the boxcar tour:

A night stop somewhere near Chemnitz, where we stood for a minute or two in the yards, heard an air-raid alarm, had the train take off suddenly like a scared rabbit, heard the guns going behind us and the motors of many planes overhead, low in the black cloudy sky.

The near-riot we had in a small town near Nuremberg when we rushed to get at a small water spigot on the station platform, were warned away by a guard, were so thirsty we paid no attention, whereupon the guard broke out his machine gun and fired a burst over us to break it up.

February, 1945

The mentality—no, worse than that—of two railroad officials at Zwichau who appeared suddenly while a lot of the guys were using the railroad yard for a toilet (there was no other) bawled out the guards, demanded that we be made to clean up the mess. And then went off all smiles and satisfied, with the present of a pack of cigarettes each.

Rumors by the millions—the Russians are 40 miles away from Berlin, Churchill-Roosevelt-Stalin meeting; we are or are not going here or there.

Odd, in the main, how quickly a man comes down to the essentials of living—eating, a place to sleep, a place to excrete waste matter, keep warm if possible. My ideas of necessities have come down even below my earlier days in Germany.

By the way, we were brought here—this is a Wehrmacht (Army) camp, not Luftwaffe—because the Germans say a regular officers' camp being built at Nuremberg is not yet complete. We are to be moved there from here in anything from eight days to three weeks—we are told. Some of the men from the other camps are already at Nuremberg, but we've learned by experience to believe nothing that we are told by these people—so we'll wait and see.

This camp seems to be (from our view of it from the train and our walk to it) very large, and contain a conglomeration of troops from every nation involved in the war. We have seen Indians, South African Negroes, Belgians, French, Bulgarians, some Italians. All are enlisted men, no officers excepting ourselves.

They put us—all 2000—in a tiny barbed wire enclosure at the extreme North end of the camp (barbed wire, incidentally, seems to be the chief crop of Germany) equipped with four small buildings—two of them dirt-floored stables—a two-hole latrine, two water spigots. Period.

Conditions are almost as bad as the boxcars, except that we aren't in motion and can get water, if we wait in line up to an hour and a half, but we were all so worn out by nightfall on arrival here that the conditions didn't make any difference. And so, sleeping all piled up like driftwood, filthy as we were, most of us managed to sleep like the dead.

February 11, 1945 (Sunday)
Moosburg

To take up the narrative a bit, we arrived in the little enclosure the evening of the 7th, but didn't quite realize until the next morning how bad the situation was.

The "barracks" where we slept so heavily had no beds, no heating facilities at all; the two lone water spigots necessitated long lines; the two-hole toilets (for 2,000 men) lines just as long; there were no facilities for cooking (and we've been weeks now without a hot meal)—and again, nothing to do.

As usual in Germany, it rained off and on, was nasty and cold, and the whitish, clayey soil got to be a peculiar sloppy consistency which we couldn't avoid tracking over the floor, our blankets and ourselves.

The Wrong Side of the Fence

During the night, all our "rank" (from colonel down to captain) and two of the old barracks complements were taken out of this compound, run through a delousing process (we were told) and taken into the main camp, where we are to stay at least for a while, and where I'm writing this.

The rest of us, filthy, wearing the same clothes we've worn steadily for two weeks, remained all day of the 8th, cold, wet, miserable—nearly half of us again really sick with stomach upsets that resulted in diarrhea and vomiting, wandering forlornly within the wire under the eyes of green-clad guards armed with odd-looking, long-barreled French rifles, kept ready-cocked.

The second night was worse—we weren't so exhausted that we could ignore the discomfort of breathing in each others' faces, sleeping atop one another, etc. During the day, the Germans brought in some of their ersatz "tea"—which none of us could drink—a few half-boiled potatoes per man, and a "soup" made of absolutely uncleaned tag-end vegetables, potato-peelings, horsemeat and mice (don't think the mice were intended as part of the menu, but they were in the soup). I ate it because it was hot, but my already bad stomach couldn't keep it down.

The next day—the 9th—was a repetition of the previous one, aggravated by rumors that we would be moved. Finally, after some 100 sick men who were unable to move were taken out, and after we stood around outside in the raw cold for some hours, they did move us—all except Bascom, who had somehow lost his POW tag and must remain behind until all the others had gone through. Another "ration"—including black bread, meanwhile had been issued under great difficulties by Applegate and Cole, among others.

These German "rations" by the way were all our food, since we had received no Red Cross supplies since boarding the train.

A short walk took us to a long plasterboard building, where we were given the most cursory search I have yet gone through; and then another hike through the pitch-dark street of the large camp brought us to the delouser—a long low building, manned by Frenchmen under German guards. I was embarrassed to find that I had forgotten so much French that I found myself sticking in German words to supply gaps in my vocabulary.

Anyway, we stripped down, put all our clothes in carts for fumigation, and as the clothes went one way, we, to our great amazement, were taken to a shower-room that had steaming hot water running from the taps.

It was lovely. It was delicious. It was—well, one must be as dirty for as long as we had been in order to appreciate it. We stayed in the shower for a half-hour, scraping up (we supplied the soap) and washing off and repeating the process, shaving, etc., until we felt almost human again.

Looking at each other, it was almost pitiful how much weight we had lost.

Incidentally, I discovered a huge patch of frostbite on the big toe and three others of my right foot. It was the first time I'd had my socks off in two weeks.

The shower over, we dressed in clothes more than a little redolent of cyanide, shouldered our packs again, and under heavy guard moved off into the Stygian darkness, under a starry but moonless sky, through what seemed to be

February, 1945

endless muddy streets and hundreds of black buildings—through three barbed-wire gates, into this so-called compound—our greatest disillusionment to date, and our worst living circumstances.

Through ankle-deep mud we slopped into a building that the Germans fondly call a barracks—a structure some 300 feet long by 40 feet wide, divided in half by two "wash" rooms consisting of a water spigot and a pump; three ridiculous "heating" stoves, 10 tiny light bulbs (for the whole building)—dank, smelly, dirty, always damp.

In it, as furniture (which could barely be distinguished in the miserable light), were 440—count 'em!—Beds, stacked up in tiers three beds high and four wide, into which we were crowded.

I don't think I can describe on paper—I haven't the right words, somehow—just how depressing these quarters are.

So damp and cold, so impossible to clean, smelling vaguely like a zoo because of the damp hay filling the mattresses, nowhere enough space to sit down to eat or read or write—and almost no light to do anything by, no facilities for cooking or even heating (there is almost no fuel available here, they say) no lockers, shelves or even pegs to hang things on.

Just four dirty walls and a pile of straw is what it amounts to.

To make it worse, we had no organization of our own—since our rank wasn't with us. So we piled into the beds amid the utmost confusion.

On the morning of the 10th, we "fell out" for the usual Appel—and, lacking organization, both on our part and on the Germans' (they still appeared not too sure of what to do with us) things were pretty much confused for about a half-hour.

A German captain, who seems to be in charge of us, got very huffy about the whole business, told us through an interpreter that if we didn't have things just so, he would make us stand at attention for two hours in the cold.

We'd had no hot food at all—except that horrible "tea" which none of us can drink.

In daylight we got a better look at our much-circumscribed world.

It consists of three more barracks exactly as dank and dirty as ours, one building housing a smelly toilet (and they'll put about 1400 men in here!)—all standing on about an acre of gooey mud, surrounded by heavy, double, barbed-wire fences.

To our West are two barracks housing Hindu troops; to the South, several barracks of American, British and New Zealand enlisted men; to the East, in a separate fenced enclosure, are two barracks containing our "rank" and the men of two of our old blocks, and to the North is a street, across which are barracks filled with Greeks, Frenchmen, Poles and what have you.

Around all is the barbed wire, sentry boxes—in the distance the ever-present pines, and to the South the spires of a church in Moosburg itself.

We understand that this campsite was used for the same purpose in the last war.

During the morning, we began to get some organization.

The Wrong Side of the Fence

After considerable shouting on both sides, ranking officers came over—by sneaking through holes in the fences—from the other compound to take charge of our group, and we began to make an effort to make things as livable as possible.

We haven't been Kriegies this long for nothing—and so some searching produced nails, odd bits of board, tin cans and whatnot, with which we set to work at making shelves, pegs, hooks, etc., on which to put away our scant possessions.

Some began laundry work, despite the cold water, some made beds, and did other household chores.

On making beds—we found the beds to be crawling with all manner of bugs, despite the Germans' vaunted cleanliness. I am already well bitten.

In the afternoon, things began to pop. It seems that Sagan's South Camp, which got here a day or so ahead of us, put up an immediate scream for the Protecting Power (the Swiss), on the ground that this was not treatment for officers—which it is not.

Not fit treatment for animals, as a matter of fact.

Anyway, since we carry considerable rank, we got immediate action—which we hope may benefit the whole camp as well as ourselves.

The Protecting Power—the Swiss—accompanied by the camp commandant, the senior British NCO, Col. Smith (now our senior officer since Gen. Vanaman and Col. Spivey left) and others, made a tour of our quarters, found (of course) they were terrible, and officially listed and made a long, and we are told, very strong protest about the march, quarters, and our treatment in general.

Results, immediately, were that we are to get just plain hot water in the morning—not ersatz tea which can't even be used for shaving; agreement to permit our own enlisted men, whom we brought with us from Sagan, to cook the "soup" which the Germans cook and issue under filthy conditions; promises to give us boilers so that we can have hot water for washing; the appearance of a load of gravel with which we made some paths through the mud of the compound yard. We wait to see other results.

Today being Sunday, our two chaplains held religious services, and then we went to work.

Fortunately, all of us have some margarine left, and with a little ingenuity and tin cans, we made a sort of stove on which—amid great clouds of greasy smoke—we were able to heat a little water and other things.

Life!

February 13, 1945 (Tuesday)
Moosburg

A queer day for me—though the first sunshine we've had since we arrived. Tomorrow is St. Valentine's Day and my wedding anniversary, and the second I've spent away from Ann. And here I won't even get mail.

February, 1945

♦ ♦ ♦

Since I last made notes here, we've progressed a bit towards living—have made some additional paths to keep out of the mud; have cleaned out the toilet ourselves (since German ideas and ours as to cleanliness differ greatly) have established a library (with 300 books—one for every sixth man); have had the other barracks filled; done some washing; made some attempts to clean up the barracks, and—with no utensils to work with—have started to work making ourselves cooking pots, pans, plates, etc., out of tin, just as we did at Sagan.

And we've learned another lesson—one in corruption.

Tammany Hall and Boss Pendergast at their palmiest never were near the corruption there is apparent here.

For a few American cigarettes, or a little coffee, or soap, one can get (through proper and established channels) anything up to and including food and a chance to escape, knives, wire-cutters, can-openers, probably firearms—anything. This from the guards themselves, as well as other prisoners who are in work parties and have access to the outside.

We've organized our foreign-language speakers into a trading corps, have made out a standard price-list, and are already in business in a large way.

Given time, we'll make out yet. But we'll all hope we're moved to a better camp. Meanwhile, through our own grapevine, we get authentic information that when we left Sagan—and when the other camps left—the Germans had only received orders to move us West, nothing else. Which would explain the apparent confusion of our march, give a good idea of the condition of the German High Command at this time. We understand that several other camps such as ours are still wandering about, and OKW itself doesn't know where they are.

Most maddening thing here is lack of news—there is no regular OKW broadcast as we had it—only "handouts" when, as and if the Germans wish to pass them out. Some of this, tonight, puts the Russ at a point North of Sagan, an shows renewed activity on the West.

One thing this trip has convinced me of—the Germans have little left—and all of that little is on the front. They are a hollow shell internally, and rotten at that. I hope.

And tonight, having shoveled gravel, washed, cooked, etc., I'm dead tired.

February 14, 1945 (Wednesday)
Moosburg

Note the noting down of the day of the week—this diary is also coming into use as a calendar, since it's becoming very hard for me to keep track of the days.

And so this is St. Valentine's Day, the 14th of February, 1945. And seven years ago on this day I stood in a church in Salt Lake City, Utah—so far away! —With Ann by my side and heard the minister marry us. Seven years ago—and what a chase I've led her since! Again I take a vow that when I get home I'll make it up to her, somehow.

The Wrong Side of the Fence

I've spent the day (what wasn't taken up in the business of living here) in running over some plans I've made for after that great day when I get home. So this digression must be excused.

To get back to our attempts to make something of a life here, I should note that we are becoming accomplished cooks in our tin-can, margarine stoves.

George (who is now eating with Post and myself due to rationing complications) made a very creditable chocolate pudding in a can yesterday, and we three combined efforts today to make a sort of fudge. Our main difficulty is that we have only one burner—and can't afford more because of the margarine consumption—and so we must start cooking hours ahead, in order to get anything done. But then we have nothing else to do at all.

Meanwhile, since today was sunshiny and comparatively warm, I shaved in cold water, and got a little exercise walking round and round our tiny compound.

The news release today told of how the Russ now in Sagan and fighting in the areas we walked through a couple of weeks ago. Still don't understand the West—no major drive seems to be under way. It appears to us that one solid blow from the West, while the Russ drive is still moving, would crumble the whole business quickly.

Anyway, we again have something to talk about.

Trading is now well organized, and all manner of things are coming in. Curiously, "D" bars, which were our standard at Sagan, are worth less here than cigarettes—one "D" bar being traded for 16 cigarettes.

Autre temps, autre mores!

February 16, 1945
Moosburg

Get letter—forms today, one per man. First chance we've had to notify the folks that we've been moved. Not much hope they'll get through, though.

As the days go on and we get more settled here, we are making entirely new friends.

Hundreds of them—and unpleasant ones.

I'm all over with bites and welts from the attention of fleas, bedbugs, lice, various other crawling (and all biting) beasts. Just what the Germans went to all the trouble of fumigating us for, when the barracks themselves are simply crawling, I'll never understand.

We try—by airing blankets and beds, by washing as well as we are able, by liberal use of German louse powder (which the bugs enjoy, as far as I can tell) to get rid of them, but to no avail.

I shall sympathize with flea-bitten animals hereafter.

Meanwhile, such another banging of tin cans, nails, wood, etc. With such a collection of makeshift tools, probably has never been seen, as the boys go about building themselves shelves, pans, pots, stoves and such things. We face

February, 1945

the problem of cooking much more seriously than do the 14,000-odd enlisted men in other sections of the camp at present. They are fed—at least it says here they are—by the Germans, and can get other food while on their work-parties, and are out of their dismal barracks a good part of the time.

But we, who are not permitted to work, are also not permitted out of our compound. I believe the Germans are watching us closer than their other prisoners. They are afraid that, because we are officers, we may succeed in organizing the camp against them.

So, daily, we receive a ration of hot soup (made out of God knows what) at noon, and a small ration of cooked (and largely rotten) potatoes, a tiny bit of cheese, plus black bread. The rest of our food consists of our Red Cross rations—issued at a half-parcel, (about three and a half pounds of food)—per man per week; and nothing on which to cook except what we can make ourselves.

Clear and sunny today—third straight like that since we've been here, and to add to the day's excitement, there was a heavy air raid somewhere close, we hearing the bombs, and seeing some of the planes as they passed overhead. Beautiful, they looked. And free. . . . . .

February 19, 1945
Moosburg

News first. Today we got a copy (smuggled in) of a Sunday newspaper, and from it we learn that the Roosevelt-Churchill-Stalin conference was held at Yalta; that the U.S. is fighting on Corregidor again; that the Russ are still going strong—Sagan has fallen. And activity increases on the West, though no major offensive under way yet.

Meanwhile, life here gets more difficult in some ways, easier in others.

We've developed some pretty fair blower-type stoves out of Klim-tins, etc., forced to it by the need of a more efficient stove and growing lack of margarine; and our over-the-fence trading has produced some fuel.

But we've been unable to rid ourselves of bugs—and I, for one, object to being considered as luncheon by any variety of bug.

The Germans thus far have made good on none of their promises to us or to the Protecting Power. We have no heat, no stoves, no hot water, no prospect of another bath, no lights, no freedom, no taking down of the fence between the compounds, they've made no attempt to clean out the toilet for a week—empty it out, I mean.

And to add to that, they've been kept in a constant state of excitement by our activities which has resulted in retaliation on their part that takes the form on continual Appels which have kept us outside in the greater cold most of the day. Fun—but very mild.

It's damned unpleasant here—but we'll make it somehow.

The Wrong Side of the Fence
February 21, 1945
Moosburg

Got to be more economical in my entries here—no prospect of any more paper when this is gone, if it goes before need for it is over. Which I keep hoping will happen.

Strange thing yesterday—we pulled a sort of sitdown strike.

Germans' fault. I mentioned not cleaning the toilet in my last note. That's what precipitated the action.

Of course, it's not really a toilet at all, just the usual pot set over a hole in the ground, which hole is emptied periodically by pumping the excrement into a tank truck (they use the feces as fertilizer).

We have one such toilet—boasting some 30 bowls—as accommodation for 1600 men. That's a lot of men. And the "toilet" was not cleaned since the day after our arrival. Yesterday, the inevitable happened—the thing overflowed. Not only all over the building, but out into the yard and all over our tiny compound.

In spite of the stench, the Germans made no attempt to do anything about it. So we simply gave up discipline, and did not fall out for Appel until ordered to do so by the Germans under threat of rifles and dogs. Once outside, we refused to fall into ranks to be counted, but simply milled around, doing nothing.

Results were immediate (we found later that two generals were inspecting the camp and the lesser officers were worried over consequences) and the Germans got into an immediate and immense flap.

They called in some 20 armed guards, and two men with dogs, and then milled about with us, arguing loudly among themselves and with our senior officers.

We just kept milling around.

Finally, a tank wagon was summoned from somewhere, started to clean out the toilet well. We then reiterated our other demands. After some two and a half hours, they promised anew to take down the fence, etc. We decided to see if they meant it in a few days, and immediately fell in orderly fashion, were counted, and went back into the barracks in good order.

The enlisted men in other compounds watched and listened in great glee, much to the chagrin of the Germans.

It shows, I think, a basic flaw in the German reasoning here. With the enlisted men, they can get away with this sort of thing—giving them a minimum for life and no more. The enlisted men are in small groups—but we are in a large one. The enlisted men are kept busy all the time—but we are not. And we are used to some privileges—are entitled to them under the Geneva Convention which they profess to adhere to (but don't).

In view of these facts, I can't understand their attitude. It's sheer stupidity for them to let things go this way. Trouble will increase in direct proportion to

February, 1945

misery among us—there have been many escapes already (though none as yet completely successful) for example.

But they followed this instance of misunderstanding this afternoon with another—distributing pamphlets urging us to join the German army to fight the Russians, promising immediate freedom (within Germany) and repatriation as soon as the Russ are defeated. I cannot believe they really expect anything from such an appeal. (See Appendix #3.)

February 26, 1945
Moosburg

Again I am amazed at the swift passage of time. But the past five days have been busy ones, what with the stupidity and disorganization of our guardians, and our almost desperate struggle to make for ourselves the wherewithal for living.

However, the news two days ago was suddenly very good—and may be getting better, since no further news has come in. Two days ago, the report was that the Allied First and Ninth Armies have opened a major offensive on the West, amid terrific poundings from the air. About this last—the air work—we are well informed. There's been an average of two or three air-raids a day in this area (North of Munich) and we can always hear the bombs exploding, and very often see the planes—P51's, B-17's, etc.

Does us good to hear and see them, though as always we are hit by the thought that the boys up there are free men, will soon be back at their own warm bases, with good food, warm beds, a decent bath—to look forward to.

And the bombings are having another possible serious effect for us. The Germans have announced that there is now on hand only enough food in Red Cross parcels to last until this coming Saturday.

After that, no more—transportation difficulties, they say, and in view of the pounding their railroads are getting, we believe them. Which isn't much help—living on the tiny and very poor rations they give us is going to be awfully thin. But, if it means the war is so nearly over as to be counted in days (as some think) we can all make it, and welcome.

As evidence of the low parcel stocks, a crazy assortment of odds-and-ends parcels, American, British, Canadian, Christmas, Invalid, were brought in today. And if anyone at home ever mentions his civilian difficulties with rationing, I shall go mad, I think, and kill him.

It's one thing to contend with difficulties with stamps and things, but when life itself depends on the rationing of a tiny bit of food—splitting a can of meat four ways, and then trying to make your share last two days—then you have something.

On the matter of wherewithal for living: I've mentioned that the Germans have provided no stoves, and no fuel and no utensils for cooking. Through our own efforts—bartering, strips of boards, cardboard, etc., we have obtained fuel of a sort on our own. But we have so little, and it is of such a nature, that we must have a means of making it into a hot, quick fire, in order to have any hope of heating even water.

Our first efforts were margarine burners, built in a hurry, but which proved to be slow and much too expensive. Then, out of tin cans, string, odd bits of wood, a few nails (all found) we constructed forced-draft burners. These burners are untold labor to build, considering the lack of tools and materials, are a bit clumsy to use, have small capacity, but are very efficient nevertheless.

And now someone—out of two Klim cans, a butter can and a salmon-tin—constructed a real gas-burner. It burns everything from paper to wood to coal down to nothing but flaky ash, and burns it without smoke, so that the burner can be used indoors. A really ingenious contraption, and so simple.

Post, George and I, like most of the men, have been heavily engaged in construction for the past five days and are now possessed of both a blower and a gas-burner, we are finally in position to provide ourselves hot meals, from soup to coffee, providing we can continue to get fuel.

Next concern is to make cooking utensils—a situation we will remedy as our supply of cans increases.

The foregoing, by the way, gives no real picture of the immense amount of labor and real ingenuity required to do these things—using table-knives for the tin shears and hammers, odd bits of iron or rock for hammers, odd-shaped cans for materials. But, it takes up time and offers considerable reward—and we have plenty of time.

The stupidity and confusion I mentioned here have taken the form of two or three Appels per day—sometimes lasting as long as three hours—during which everyone from German privates to captains and colonels count us, working separately and in groups to count the same men, then standing in large bunches gesticulating and arguing in an attempt to agree on the count; in continued evidence that they have no intention of doing any of the things they've promised; in not permitting use of the latrine (which is outside the barracks) during air-raids that sometimes last for hours; in providing no heat, etc.

A prime example occurred two days ago. Two days before that, our complaints about the bedbugs, lice and fleas, having reached a new high, they took the 800 men out of two of the barracks, moved them to the enclosure where we were first held (which we have come to know as the Snake Pit), held them there two days while their barracks were deloused and sent the men themselves back through the delouser and the shower.

Two days ago it was our turn. For some reason or another, we couldn't go to the Snake Pit directly, but had to go from our enclosure to another directly behind it, built to house a group of French prisoners. So, all packed, we stood outside on a cold morning, getting thoroughly wet under a heavy damp snowfall, for more than two hours, were counted at least four times, then walked to the tents. They counted us again there, and turned us into the tents themselves—

these long, damp low affairs, built on the ground and filled with damp wood-shaving "straw" being the housing provided for the French, in winter.

There we stayed for about five hours, without heat (I got a sore throat out of it) until suddenly came another order to move.

We did—right back to our own compound. We were counted there three times, and then within an hour were ordered to fall out again for still another Appel—which effectively ruined our preparations for heating meals and our dispositions, let alone health.

In our absence, our barracks had been sprayed with sulphur—which did no good at all—I got more bugs' bites that night than on any previous one.

War is really hell on this end.

Though I'm learning something else—nothing is so bad it couldn't be worse. Those Frenchmen in those tents will be a lot worse off than we are, even as bad as these dank barracks are.

February 28, 1945
Moosburg

I knew that, given time and tin cans enough, somebody would build something approaching a real stove.

I did it myself.

Not that I can take the entire credit by any means, since the original gas-burner stove was not my invention. But I discovered, by adding flues, that I can make the one fire heat three separate spots at once. So, I added a couple of cans and presto! (to my own great surprise) we have a real stove, capable of heating three dishes at once. And on a surprisingly small amount of fuel—two or three sticks of wood.

I am childishly pleased with the thing, and will stand quite happily fooling with it for any amount of time. On it, George, Post and I have managed to get completely hot meals—hot potatoes, meat and coffee, as well as some quite successful toasted sandwiches, tiny puddings, etc.

Although a lot of trouble, the stove makes the difference between something approaching decent living and an animal-like existence. Cole and Applegate, Eatinger and Webb, most of the others, have now constructed similar apparatuses.

Now, the problem remains whether we'll continue to cook anything—whether we'll get any parcels or not. Rumors are running wild on the subject now. As always.

Chapter 10

♦

March, 1945

March 4, 1945
Moosburg

Having a hard time writing tonight—gave myself a nasty cut on my right thumb while cutting up wood for our little stove.

The wood situation, by the way, is becoming acute, since the Germans issued orders prohibiting our approaching the fences, over which came a good bit of our bartered material. So, since no wood has been coming in by this means, and since the Germans' ration of wood consists of nothing, we are looking with hungry eyes on any piece of wood at all. Hot meals of some sort are of more importance to us than many other comforts—and we have started whittling away the beds for use as fuel.

Of course, the food situation may resolve itself very quickly, if no more Red Cross parcels arrive; the Germans have announced that they issued the last of the parcels on hand yesterday. If this is true—and with the immense damage to railroads by the daily air raids (we understand that for days last week no trains were able to operate at all in this and the Munich area), it can well be that we will be able to get only the scant German-issued rations.

And it brings another problem. That of tobacco. Our only supplies of that come in the Red Cross parcels. This will be a serious loss—for tobacco is more than smoking material to us—it is also money.

But the continuance of the big American-Canadian drive on the West, plus the Russ on the East, makes even this miserable existence possible.

Any continuing the lesson about things being worse elsewhere, we learn from the Red Cross representative that the camps at Nuremberg are worse off than we—living in tents, no Red Cross rations for weeks now. But our main topic continues to be food.

March 6, 1945 (Tuesday)
Moosburg

Cold, cold, cold. Snow and rain, and my shoes have been wet for days. Haven't had a bath in a month now—haven't even had my clothes all off at the same time. We do our best towards washing under the single tap, but can't do much with cold water, and it's literally taking your life in your hands to strip down and expose yourself completely to this biting cold.

The food situation is really bad—we thought it might be, but didn't really know.

Most of us are now completely out of Red Cross rations. Post, George and I, for instance, have nothing left but a few bouillon cubes, a little salt and a part of a can of honey.

We can and will live on the Germans' rations—but bare living is all we can do, on an issue of hot water in the morning, a cup of soup at noon, about five potatoes and an occasional tiny morsel of cheese at night. All this, plus a sixth of a loaf of black bread—about five thin slices.

A damned thin time, and the lack of food only accentuates the craving for it. Our every waking thought turns to food—quantities of food, all the food we have ever eaten or hope to eat.

It's maddening, but we can't keep our minds off it. Every conversation turns to this, inevitably. And one thing is certain—when we get out of here and back where we can, none of us will ever go hungry again, even if we must steal or do anything else to get it.

Lack of parcels is quickly cutting down on another activity—tinwork. No cans, no work.

Our only real hope now is the news, which continues good—the offensive on the West having reached the Rhine at Neuss, according to the last much-edited OKW release we got, and seems to be going ahead. Lord, Lord, how we hope this will finish it!

Speaking of food, Post, George, Eatinger and I finished our "lunch" of a cup of stringbean soup and two thin half-slices of bread a while ago, and then spent an hour happily planning a banquet for members of the combine when we're released.

We figure we must hold the banquet on this side of the water, for once in the States, there'll be no gathering this gang again.

Anyway, we planned an elaborate meal—starting with wine, clear consommé (with noodles), salad, fish course, meat course, vegetable course, desserts, coffee, ice-cream—all to be accompanied by other wines, hot rolls and butter, coffee, etc. To be followed by a two-hour period of rest and relaxation, after which mixed drinks and small sandwiches until either we or the necessary money run out.

Childish as it may seem to anyone who has not been a POW, we were entirely serious in our discussion. And we made ourselves forget our miserable condition for a while. Which is justification enough.

March 11, 1945 (Sunday)
Moosburg

Once again, bless the Red Cross!!

Germany is starving—having announced that further ration cuts will go into effect in the second week in April. But we are getting parcels again.

The Wrong Side of the Fence

As I noted, we ran out of parcels last Saturday, and the past week, on nothing but German rations has been awfully thin going indeed. This, coupled with the nasty, cold, raw weather, has made it hard to maintain morale, despite the startling news that the Allies are across the Rhine.

Anyway, three days ago the story ran through the camp that 72 carloads of parcels were standing in the Moosburg freight yards. The story was true. We were told that this camp has now been made the distribution center for all POW food, things look better. Only eight cars remained here, the others going to Nuremberg, etc. But eight carloads is enough for two weeks at half-parcels, and we have been assured that a fleet of 100 Red Cross trucks will be running very soon, carrying more parcels from Switzerland.

Impossible to describe to anyone who has not been so desperately hungry what a blessing the addition of a little powdered milk, chocolate, tinned meats, can be.

◆ ◆ ◆

Last night we had our first "end of the war" excitement.

A wild rumor, starting God knows where, swept the whole camp, including the enlisted men over the wire.

Our reactions were peculiar. Imagine what such a thing means to us, let alone to the rest of the world. It means freedom for us, home to us, food to us, clothes to us—life, to us.

And yet, war has been so long a matter of course to us, that we can't quite imagine its end. So we half-believed, wanting to believe, but not daring to.

Of course it was false, but I fully expect several more before the real thing comes.

And I am now firmly convinced that the next two months will see the end of it—at least as far as we are concerned. I do not look for the end to come formally, but rather with a more or less complete disintegration and an overrunning of the country by our troops and the Russ. First real notice to us may very well be the arrival of paratroops or something like them at the gates.

Most of us are sure the end is near—the most optimistic placing this date in mid-April. And while we wait, we are like the children on the night before Christmas, with "visions of sugarplums"—as we talk over and savor our plans for going home, the future, and particularly the food we'll eat. I can't emphasize this insistence on food enough—anyone who has been really hungry for long may understand.

Meanwhile, although they make no effort to get us baths or do anything else they've promised, the Germans go ahead with construction around us—construction of fences.

They have already built no less than three barbed-wire fences around the compound, and are continually adding wire in odd places. Newest is from the East fence to the toilet. Ask me why.

Post and I have been heavily engaged in tinwork in the past two days, extending our stove for George (who has again taken over cooking duties), to

March, 1945

accommodate a fourth member of our eating group—Harold Farthing, Asheville, N.C., George's pilot. In order to cook for four, we had to add another burner to the stove, make additional plates, cups, etc.

March 14, 1945 (Wednesday)
Moosburg

Peculiar air-raid yesterday—peculiar in German reaction, anyway.

A clear, sunny day, and most of us were gratefully soaking in the sunshine when we heard sirens far off. Oddly, we were not immediately chased into the barracks. In a few minutes a P51 came roaring over, not 100 feet high, waggling his wings at us, playing in the sky.

He looked as good as the Stars and Stripes up there. For about a half-hour he swooped around us. Not a single German plane appeared—the sky was empty.

One lone machine gun burst was fired from the ground, and he answered with a short burst. And that was all.

Then we heard the dull, heavy rumble of the bombers coming and were chased inside—but from the windows we saw the 17's and 24's heading Northeast, and shortly the ground shook with a whole wing's bomb-pattern hitting.

Today, too, there were contrails all over the sky as six P38's flew about. But no alarm, and no German planes.

But on the ground, the Germans are building strong earthwork pillboxes at each corner of our compound—for what we can only guess. Doesn't mean too much—they do these things according to the book. We remember that at Sagan they were repairing windows in the barracks the day we left.

New continues excellent. Filtered OKW reports we get now admit that Allies have a bridgehead across the Rhine at Remagen, and are along the river from Bonn Northwards. German newspapers daily print long articles—some of them acutely enough written—explaining the military situation, minimizing Allied and Russ successes though making no attempt to disguise the gravity of the situation, explaining the further obstacles the Germans will throw in the way of advances. But they hold out no hope of victory or much else, and we wonder how long the people will hold on in view of this situation, plus increasing strictures on food.

Tried my most ambitious tinwork project to date in the past two days—construction of a coffee-pot out of seven odd-sized cans. Again to my amazement, it works. Leaked at first, but a pudding cooked in it sealed it well enough.

Through the combined efforts of Post and myself, we are now possessed of three eating plates, a frying pan, another odd cooking pan, a coffeepot, two cooking pots, and both the gas stove and the blower for cooking.

March 24, 1945 (Saturday)
Moosburg

Saturday, and no baths. They had promised us hot showers today, but cancelled because the camp records finally arrived from Sagan, and we had a picture-parade instead—a long process during which each man is called up to a table and compared with German photos taken when we went through Dulag Luft. A long, silly business, during which we were kept outside from 9 A.M. until nearly 2 P.M.

But it was almost worth it. The day was clear and cloudless and the sun was actually hot, and we had an air show.

By the hundreds, the B-24's came over—beautiful silver fish against the deep blue of the sky. Formation after formation, with the fighter cover flashing over and through and around them like a school of minnows. The noise of their engines sounded as loud as it used to back in England, when the group and wing assembled over our base.

They were unmolested—no sign of flak or German fighters anywhere. Somehow, the sight of them there, so purposeful and so evidently in complete command of the air, was the clincher to me that the end of this business will come soon. The news bears it out—the bridgehead holds, Patton has reached the Rhine, Montgomery is readying something big.

As to baths—never realized before what it is to be really dirty. My skin is all dry and flaky from it, my hair if filthy, I cannot even get my hands clean in this icy water. I'm looking forward to a bath as I look forward to plenty of food.

We're on full parcels now (with the trainloads that arrived some time ago), but we are still hungry. The German rations have been cut to less than half of the small amount they were—we get potatoes three days a week now; cheese three days, no salt. Miss the bulk the potatoes provide.

Note: Always thought our own Army not very much to look at in the matter of enlisted men's uniforms, but never saw a raunchier looking lot than the Germans. Particularly of late, when they have been appearing in all sorts of tag-end clothes, even including captured Allied uniform coats with German epaulets.

Fleas and bedbugs getting worse with the warmer weather. Dammit.

March 27, 1945
Moosburg

Things in the news are happening so fast I feel a distinct urgency to write this down as quickly as possible, because this thing may blow up any minute now.

OKW, surprisingly frank, yesterday put the Third Army beyond Frankfurt-am-Main—and today even further beyond and putting out prongs North and South, towards us. The First Army has broken out of its bridgehead to the East, and Montgomery is across and strongly moving.

The thing looks more and more as I envisioned it (note pat on back!)—a swift military occupation in the wake of a rapid breakup of the German army. I can't quite visualize how it will come to us, but I rather expect to wake up any

March, 1945

morning to find that the Germans have turned over the operation of this camp to us as the only Allied officers here, and either decamped en masse or remained here for protection.

Certainly their treatment of us indicates the end—they have finally permitted our enlisted men to take over the kitchen, are organizing wood walks, etc.

German news is again surprisingly frank, but has assumed a generally plaintive air. The reports filtered in to us are very sketchy, but articles in the daily papers are full of explanations for the Allied successes, tributes to German troops, recriminations for bombing of cities, daily new assurances of measures that will control the advances—all hidden in a mass of verbiage that reads clearly as nothing but desperation to anyone familiar with publicity measures. It's amazing they hang on even now. In any case, it isn't long—so close now I can taste it.

Incident—yesterday, a guard shot a South African Negro private, working on the fence in our compound. Right through the head. No apparent reason, no consequences to the guard. Our own information set-up has already painted a pretty bad record for the guards here—something like an average of five prisoner deaths per day—from gunshot wounds.

With the imminence of the end, with the operation of a fleet of Red Cross trucks which assure a constant food supply—and even more our almost insane craving for a full meal, just once—we have embarked on another lunacy. Which is attempt after attempt by individuals to eat an entire Red Cross parcel in one day.

No use to comment on the idiocy of the attempts—particularly where the food cannot be replaced. Eight pounds of food, all highly concentrated, is a tremendous lot to eat in eight hours even under normal conditions. And in our present state—I must have lost 20 pounds since we left Sagan, for instance—it is an overload of no mean proportions.

No one has been able to do it yet, but the temptation is very great.

Another item of life here is the growth of trading by barter among us. Brings the point of money to prominence—so difficult to evaluate items in terms of others. How much is a "D" bar worth in terms of tobacco? Or eggs in terms of oatmeal? Or Spam in terms of Corned Beef? Or a sweater in terms of food?

Chapter 11

◆

April, 1945

April 1, 1945
Moosburg

Easter Sunday. Dawned bright and clear after two days of rain during which I was quite literally sick as a dog. Couldn't hold anything on my stomach—didn't even try to eat a solid meal for two days. Our doctor (also a prisoner)—working under miserable conditions with few medicines—told me it was a combination of run-down condition (the bugs make sleeping a real problem), poor food, intestinal flu. He filled me full of pills and advice, all of which worked.

Which brings up a point—what really bad shape I and most of the others really are in. We are more than thin—we are emaciated, skin and bone, most of us. We have not recovered from the march, the food we've gotten has just about enabled us to hold our own and no more.

Now, on full parcels (but with radically less bulk ration from the Germans), we have a little more food. So most of us have been like kids loose in a candy store—busying ourselves day-long with the preparation of sweets.

Went to church service today and was much affected. But I'm convinced it's my last such service here. Because the news is tremendous—our troops are overrunning Germany at a pace that seems to be just as fast as our armor can move—one column is already nearing Nuremberg and within 70 or 80 miles of here.

So the end—and home—is very close today.

I'm convinced the Germans are thoroughly confused by now, and are hanging on out of habit. They've been under discipline so long that when the top command is lacking they continue their jobs through habit—they don't know what else to do.

April 9, 1945 (Monday)
Moosburg

Should make mention of the rumor situation.

As usual in any Army camp, rumors are hot and heavy, but even more so here because we have another source than our own imaginings—the enlisted men of all nations (including German) who work around the camp. Many of

April, 1945

the rumors we get are true, if sometimes early. I fully expect that the war's end may come to us that way—somehow.

A now-authenticated rumor started two weeks ago, to the effect that the Sagan camps that went to Nuremberg (West, South and North camps)—some six or seven thousand men—would be moved here, to get them out of the track of the Allied advance now sweeping toward the town. Yesterday, we heard some 2,000 sick and wounded had already arrived here, and the Germans erected huge tents in our already overcrowded, tiny compound, to house more. We may yet see Dave, if he's in that crowd.

Addition of another 2,000 or more men here will <u>really</u> crowd things. In our total area of little more than an acre of ground, there is already almost no place to walk or set up for cooking (which we do outside when possible because of the smoke in the barracks)—Coney Island on the Fourth has nothing on this place for mobs.

We have only two toilets—some 45 bowls in all (with those in the compound next to us which has now been opened to us) to serve all these men now, and the toilets are already filling up and overflowing almost daily. We have now one water tap to each 250 men—double it, and I shudder to think what the answer will be.

Meanwhile, the Germans seem bent on making this an all-American camp. Yesterday they moved out all the Frenchmen from the tents south of us, and moved in a bunch of American GI's. The French went to Augsburg, we understand.

In the barracks next to us on the West—once occupied by the Hindus—they have now housed a bunch of Australian and New Zealand officers, brought from some camp on the Rhine near Strasbourg, according to information yelled over the fence.

And I am still at a loss to understand the German mentality. They have now lost, in addition to all their proud conquests, more than a third of their own country; countless men and equipment, all of their industry. And yet they keep on with it—and hang onto us grimly, as well. Who knows what the end will be? Anyway, I've given up predictions.

Weather turned fine and warm again in the past two days—a grateful thing.

And we've now been two months without a proper bath. Tie that. Just can't get clean in this icy fluid they call water here.

April 10, 1945
Moosburg

Yesterday, after I got through writing at about 3 P.M., got very quickly into the realm of the fantastic—no other word can describe it.

At about 3 P.M. the new men started to come into our compound—these being from South Camp which has been here, but in another part of the camp. Two more of my classmates were among them: Bill Perkinson of Baltimore, with whom I worked on the camp paper back in San Antonio (Lord! That was

The Wrong Side of the Fence

nearly two years ago), and Don Fisher, who was in my flight back at navigation school. Fisher's arrival brings to five the number of men here not only of my class and school, but of my <u>barracks</u> who are now in this camp. With Dave First, who is also down in one of the camps, it makes six of the same outfit down, and POW's.

Unlucky—or lucky.

Also incoming were Curt Goza, a pilot who went through phase training with us at El Paso, and some of his crew.

For most of us, then—both the men coming in and those here—the whole thing assumed a sort of carnival atmosphere—an old home week, a homecoming. And the circus-like tents in the background, the bundles the boys carried, the ceaseless milling around occasioned by the fact that no one knew where to go, and no one had any place to sit down, plus a perfectly beautiful spring day. Plus a couple of dray teams driven by German enlisted men with big handlebar mustaches—all added to it.

And the top was a perfect series of groups of B-24's that flew directly overhead and bombed a target somewhere South of us, but within our sight. There was no opposition but some light flak—which got one plane, bursting into flames—poor fellows.

The rest of that day and night, and today are proof enough that the Germans have lost their grip.

They have no control over us at all—we have overrun the warning rails, and are industriously taking apart slit trenches, fences and any other things in sight, for firewood. Germans couldn't even hold Appel this morning—too many men milling around.

Meanwhile, though, conditions are fast approaching the intolerable. We get rumors that the Germans have declared this area to be "open", that these new men are to be moved into barracks to the North of us.

But the Allies are only 80 miles away, to the North of us near Stuttgart. Hope!

April 13, 1945 (Friday)

Got word today of the death of President Roosevelt.

It was shocking enough of itself—he was one of the world's great men—but it made me realize as almost nothing else how far out of the stream of the world we are.

Meanwhile the news continues to be in the terrific class—our maps (manufactured at great cost and in great secrecy) showing Germany almost cut in two near Berlin. These stupid fools continue to put up a feeble resistance and lose their lives, despite the fact that the war has been over to all intents and purposes for several weeks. My own view (and that of many others) is that we are now only sweating out the arrival of someone to take us out.

April, 1945

Despite the German promises of enlargement of the compound, South camp is still with us, and we are unbelievably crowded. Our one toilet has overflowed twice now, with resultant stench and filth.

Stragglers from the group that were at Nuremberg also are coming in—some of them with fantastic stories of their march down, living on the countryside—including the story that, though many tried to escape, they were halted by the Red Cross, which told them that German SS troops were following the exodus and had shot some stragglers.

Personally, I seem to grow hungrier and hungrier as time goes on. Suppose it's because we are getting almost no bulk food now. I would give anything I have, though, for food if I could get it.

April 16, 1945 (Monday)

One fantastic thing after another keeps piling up to make this the most unbelievable section of our experience to date.

South camp is still here, but yesterday the Germans moved out all the ground-forces personnel on what they call "Commando"—work parties on farms—and as these men left the camp, they were allowed to come quite freely to our fences, trading any possession (including civilian type bread, flour, wheat, other foods) for cigarettes, which in turn can trade to civilians outside.

With such articles, also, came the most complete and weird assortment of pliers, wire cutters, hammers, wrenches, etc., imaginable. And the oddest thing was that these things were traded with the complete approval of the German guards, who even went so far as to assist in the trading and hand things over the fences.

Meanwhile, all the wood in the slit trenches in our compound, all the small fences the Germans have so laboriously been building, and even one of the main fences have utterly disappeared—removed by us during the night and in broad daylight, not by the Germans. For fuel.

The boys have really run wild. They've cut holes in the main fence between us and the British just West of us—and we and the British have been visiting back and forth, trading madly for battle-jackets and such, and getting acquainted. Other holes have been cut in other fences.

Held very impressive, simple memorial service for President Roosevelt Saturday. Taps, as always sweetly sad, sound odd here.

April 19, 1945 (Thursday)

Got to hold this to brief now—running close on paper. Just to note that the Allies are in Nuremberg, and we again under tension about moving. Though why we should, or to what purpose I wouldn't know. Latest rumors have Himmler a suicide, paratroops at Innsbruck. Boys keep drifting in from Nuremberg with strange stories of escapes, picnics on the road, etc. Among them Al Catlin—Greenquist's pilot. Got a British battle jacket today in a swap for my year-old flying jacket. Fence between us and British compound comes

The Wrong Side of the Fence

down (officially) tomorrow. With warm weather we are living outdoors as much as possible. Air shows every day.

April 22, 1945 (Sunday)

Odd days, these. Allies get closer to us, we have big air shows every day, we overrun the camp more and more, tension over possible move grows, I have tea with British officers, remnants of other camps, plus British, French, Polish, etc., keep drifting in until we must be nearly 15,000 officers strong now. Dave First arrives with additional fantastic stories of the march from Nuremberg. Also arrived is a new commanding officer (for us), Col. Good, oldest ranking officer in U.S. Army.

And another coincidence. Back last November in one of my first letters, Mother asked me to look up Bob Jensen, tell him his wife had a baby. I didn't know him, and he was not in our camp—so gradually forgot. Today, Bob Jensen introduced himself to me. A Bombardier, he went down in Austria in August, has been in West camp. Incidentally—I gave him first news of the baby, but couldn't tell him its sex.

April 26, 1945 (Thursday)

Events have been piling up for us very fast, and the tempo is increasing.

Most important for us was the announcement, read officially two days ago, that the German and Allied governments had agreed that POW's would no longer be moved in the face of Allied advances. This was followed up yesterday by the word—again officially—that orders had been issued to German commanders, at their discretion, to decamp, leaving only skeleton forces to maintain utilities, and turn over security and operation of the camps to senior Allied officers in the camps.

Although this issue has not been officially approved by the German commandant here, we are already making plans for the eventuality, which will see a Britisher—Wing Commander Willetts—as Senior Allied Officer.

This, coupled with evidence that the Allied Command is really concerned about us—which evidence includes a pamphlet printed in German dropped in yesterday's air raid warning against mistreatment of war prisoners—gives us high hopes of quick evacuation.

The war is nearly over—we are almost completely surrounded by Allied armies advancing from the West, North and Northeast on Munich—the Seventh Army was only 40 miles away yesterday, and we can hear their guns. Heavy explosions—probably demolition by the Germans, going on continually, too.

Meanwhile, I'm learning a bit. Count the time not completely wasted so long as I can learn something about the other fellow. And since the camp is now full of officers from every army—even including some Bulgars who came in last night and told me they had been "invading Germany"—I've made a point of pumping them for all the information I can get about their homelands,

April, 1945

themselves, their viewpoints. Even my halting French is becoming less halting as I use it more and more—thus probably completing the total decline of the language as a civilized tongue.

Most of my conversations have been with the British contingent—New Zealanders, South Africans, Australians—who have proved fine fellows, and from whom I have learned an amazing lot, both personally and in comportment here. Many of them have been prisoners three to five years, yet they are neat as a pin, in high spirits. Get a big kick out of them—have no doubt they get as much out of me and my friends.

April 28, 1945 (Saturday)
Two more days passed—and I suppose they've gone quickly enough for most outside, but they are two of the slowest days I ever hope to live through.

We are tired of waiting for the release we now expect hourly, and our nerves are wearing thin with the strain. We find ourselves snapping at one another over the most trivial things, have to exercise real control to keep from actual blows. For instance, yesterday I got so highly incensed over a discussion as to what we should do to prepare a can of Spam that I had to walk off. Childish, but real.

Yesterday, the Allies were within 25 miles of Munich, and closer to us. Hard to understand why it takes them so long to get here.

Meanwhile, the Germans have been moving out rapidly from here—heading South in companies and larger groups, until there are virtually no Germans left in camp.

Yesterday at 3 P.M. we officially took over the camp in its internal administration. And for the first time, we saw our own men as guards—though unarmed—posted in and around the camp to maintain order and protect property we will need.

The German guard system has disappeared completely—some of our men have even gotten dressed in uniform (American uniform), gotten through the gates and into Moosburg itself.

Yesterday also, I got a hot shower—first in three months, nearly, a bonus for our taking over the camp. Also, I'm eating my watch. Mentioned some time ago it was broken, and most of the jewels had fallen out. But I swapped it to a Russian for some chocolate and cigarettes and bread. The Poles, Russians, etc., are crazy to buy anything in the way of jewelry which has intrinsic value, since money means nothing in Europe and Germany now.

I'll chance now saying what I've not said before—we have now, and have had since I've been a prisoner and before, our own radio receivers, which have enabled us to get news, comments and orders from our side.

Just how these sets were brought in, assembled, and concealed against all the German efforts to find them (they were the objects of most of the searches—the Germans knew we must have them) is another story, one I cannot tell. Never attempted to find out—I couldn't tell because I didn't know.

The Wrong Side of the Fence

But we did and do have it. I've left mention of it out of these notes so far, for fear the Germans might pick up the information in a search. Not much danger of that now.

April 29, 1945 (Sunday)
Moosburg (9 A.M.)

All last night heavy explosions around us. Today started with a buzz-job by two P51's.

Then started the explosions, and then—for the first time—recognizable small arms fire, which has increased all morning, coming closer and closer to us.

11 A.M.

It's now 11 A.M., and we are back in the war.

The Germans here (SS troops, we hear) are stupidly putting up some sort of resistance.

As usual, we Americans (with a lot of the British) milled around all morning while the firing and excitement increased—until suddenly bullets began to whine through the compounds. Don't know which side was firing, but it was no place or time to argue the point. We all hit the dust (including me—very fast too) without ceremony—two Colonels scrabbling right along with me on their bellies to get behind a building. Three men wounded. Just what is outside we don't know, but our boys, anyway.

Plenty exciting—I'll keep this page open.

12:15 P.M.

FOR US THE WAR IS OVER!!!

The battle around Moosburg is finished, and the American flag—our own Old Glory—is flying over the town, from the remaining tower of the church.

I can't describe emotion here. Tears close, and no one ashamed.

An anniversary for us too—10 months, to the day, since we came down in Holland.

4 P.M.

What a session this has been.

Immediately the flag went up over Moosburg, the camp here burst out in colors too—the French Tricolor, the British Union Jack, the Red Flag of Russian, and Greek, Bulgar, Croat, Italian—other banners, all carefully saved for the occasion, it seems.

Within half an hour, as the sounds of firing behind us and around us faded in the distance, we suddenly saw a surge of brown uniforms on the road South of us—between us and the town. And in another half-hour the end really came for us, with the arrival—to the accompaniment of tremendous cheering—of a

April, 1945

monstrous Sherman tank, chuffing down the prison street in the wake of a jeep carrying our two senior officers—Commander Willetts and Col. Good.

And so, again, "Pour vous, la Guerre est fini."

Since then, the place has been swarming with our own soldiers—this is the Third Army, by the way—in tin hats and carrying sidearms—and it's good to see them. How good, I can't put into words.

My own reaction is peculiar enough. I keep telling myself it's over—that I'm free, that I'm going home. And I find I'm not moved too much, hard put to believe it.

I've been expecting it too long.

Rumors flying thick and fast—to the effect that we start moving out tonight. So, with no further thought of saving, we're eating heartily tonight. Uncle Sam brings the food now.

8 P.M.

Not moving out tonight, apparently. Just finished supper—for us a hearty meal and I feel a bit heavy. Clouded over in the afternoon, but sun going down in a real blaze of glory now.

Souvenir hunters already busy acquiring German helmets, knives, etc.

Chapter 12

♦

May, 1945

May 2, 1945 (Wednesday)
Moosburg

This thing has developed so fast and has gotten so big as to get to the limit of my power of description, and my own powers of belief.

The battle, such as it was, was over Sunday night. By Monday afternoon the camp was swarming with jeeps, trucks, tanks, ambulances, even two Red Cross girls—and with more food than any of us has seen in Germany; Tuesday, General Patton arrived, spoke to us (3 words), moved on with the troops; Tuesday night we had an issue of real WHITE bread (which tastes like cake to us) and by today they are ready to start evacuating the camp. Exactly when we leave (except that it will be in the next day or two), we don't know, nor where we go.

But we have been told we'll be moved out by airplane. So, it's "home again, and home again—America for me!", and I can't paint the prospect that holds out for us.

Meanwhile, we have been running nearly wild, like a pack of children, swarming into town against orders, gathering everything from German uniforms and weapons to autos, horses, pigs, sheep, etc., as souvenirs and food.

And with the appearance of good old American plenty, we've done something we've wanted to do for a long time—invited guests to dinner: Tony Patterson and Derrick Powrie—two New Zealanders with whom we've become very friendly.

So this narrative comes near to a close—only a day or two now, one way or the other. And I'm glad to see it so.

Meanwhile, the troops have brought in something else that is almost meat and drink to us. Newspapers and magazines, fresh (within 12 days) from the States, and the first we've seen since we've been prisoners. And we ourselves lost little time acquiring radios (stolen from the town, of course) on which we can get English-spoken broadcasts, music.

May, 1945

Friday, May 4, 1945
Moosburg

This thing lingers on a bit. They've made a start evacuating us, but weather, red tape, transportation difficulties, have held up the move.

THIS waiting is almost worse than the other, for this is really the home stretch.

Some of us—myself, George, Post included—have availed ourselves of ample opportunity to go for long exploratory walks in the countryside, and found it lovely. Others, a little disgustingly, have been doing some mild but effective looting in search of souvenirs.

Cole got what was probably the biggest surprise of the war yesterday, when his brother Gordon, a lieutenant of Artillery, walked into the barracks. They hadn't seen each other for over three years—just luck that Gordon, attached to the 7th Army in this area—ran in on the chance his brother would be here.

Wednesday, May 9, 1945
Manching, Germany

This is the last entry I shall make in this diary—the last note of any kind I expect to make in Germany.

Because we're going home today.

Not directly of course—but to a collection camp near LeHavre, France, thence by boat.

But to me, today is the day I start the home trail—the big C47's that will take us out are landing on this former German airfield now.

They'll be taking me back to Ann, to the folks—civilization, the gentler ways of gentler days.

Only in memory will I ever again eat or drink or cook in a tin can; only in memory live in a filthy, flea-ridden barracks; march in leaking shoes and carry a heavy pack in 24° below zero weather; be held behind barbed wire.

We were brought to this place by truck convoy two days ago, dumped here on the field to await transport out. Discovered that the field, some four miles South of Ingolstadt on the Danube, was a former German Cadet training base, and there are literally hundreds of German planes scattered about in the heavy woodland all about. Some of our still incorrigible souvenir hunters have been having a field day.

The waiting here has been hard on us—we've been watching the 47's fly over for two days, taking out other men.

The war ended officially yesterday, but caused hardly a ripple among us—it HAS been over for us.

But now the planes are coming in for us. Cole and Post, by accident of name, will go in other planes—our first trip apart in a year and a half. I haven't

The Wrong Side of the Fence

found Dave as yet, though I hope he's safe and well, and there are many loose ends to tie up, memories to cherish.

But the main thing is — — —

I'M GOING HOME TODAY!

◆ ◆ ◆

Departed Germany 11:13 A.M., May 9, 1945.

Not long after release, Halmos meets with colleagues at Engineering News Record (McGraw Hill) in New York. Left to right: Halmos (in uniform); Van Tuyl Boughton (senior editor); Waldo Bowman (editor in chief); Edward Cleary (managing editor). Note difference in appearance of Halmos as compared to frontispiece—shows loss of weight, etc., even though when Halmos appeared here, he had been in Allied hands for a couple of weeks of decent food and medical attention.

WESTERN UNION

CLASS OF SERVICE

This is a full-rate Telegram or Cable-gram unless its deferred character is indicated by a suitable symbol above or preceding the address.

1201

SYMBOLS

DL=Day Letter
NL=Night Letter
LC=Deferred Cable
NLT=Cable Night Letter
Ship Radiogram

A. N. WILLIAMS
PRESIDENT

The filing time shown in the date line on telegrams and day letters is STANDARD TIME at point of origin. Time of receipt is STANDARD TIME at point of destination

(OB)

1945 JUN 2 PM 2 11

N103 43 GKVT=WUX WASHINGTON DC 2 145P

MRS ELIZABETH A HALMOS=

33-19 166TH ST QUEENS NY=

THE CHIEF OF STAFF OF THE ARMY DIRECTS ME TO INFORM YOU THAT YOUR HUSBAND 2/LT HALMOS EUGENE E JR IS BEING RETURNED TO THE UNITED STATES WITHIN THE NEAR FUTURE AND WILL BE GIVEN AN OPPORTUNITY TO COMMUNICATE WITH YOU UPON ARRIVAL=

:J A ULIO THE ADJUTANT GENERAL.

2/LT.

THE COMPANY WILL APPRECIATE SUGGESTIONS FROM ITS PATRONS CONCERNING ITS SERVICE

Afterword

Just to bring this story to a conclusion, it might be worth saying that the entire crew returned home, safely and reasonably well, at the end of hostilities.

I visited with some of them—notably the Moos and Hart families, after my own return (when I took my wife on a long-promised "Honeymoon" trip to Niagara Falls and elsewhere) and was advised that all had "made it."

Many years later, I had occasion to contact the three officers: Cole, Post and Dave Smart—and found that Cole had returned to Eastman Kodak in Rochester, married, produced three sons and some grandchildren. Post passed away about 1991 (at the age of about 74), but his wife, Irene, remained in Pendleton, Indiana, with three sons (one of whose birth I recorded). Smart had returned to Kansas, took over his father's construction-equipment sales organization, and later sold it. He had married and divorced (after the birth of a daughter), has since remarried, and is now living near Topeka.

Appendix 1

♦

Further Details about Interrogations

Thinking back on this questioning—and on some other interrogations I went through, many months and years later—I have concluded that despite my determination not to do so, I might have told the questioners something after all, or at least confirmed some of their information.

Having covered police matters for many years as a news reporter, I was—and am—certainly familiar with the basic techniques: try to get the person talking about anything, then tie him up in knots and probably get some real information, when you can catch him in a lie, or an obvious omission.

If you don't believe that a man gets to feeling very stupid, sitting there for a couple of hours or so, answering questions such as "what color is your mother's hair?" or "do your feet hurt?", or things like that, with the prescribed "my name is so-and-so, my rank is so-and-so, my serial number is so-and-so"—you are very wrong. The temptation to answer some of these questions directly is very strong. After all, what real help could it be to the enemy's war information if you agree that your feet do hurt, or that your mother's hair is blonde?

But maybe I told the man something anyway—by some involuntary reaction to his statements or questions. For example, I was really astonished at the enormous amount of information he had about me personally—and what he seemed to know about the military outfit I had been assigned to. He rattled off names of officers that I knew had only been assigned to certain posts within the few days before we took off on that final mission—plus other information that I figured he couldn't have obtained unless he had some sources of information within the outfit—or within headquarters itself.

So, maybe I blinked, or showed surprise or something as he read off some of his stuff—thus I might well have confirmed the accuracy of some of his information.

Again, as I recall some of this, I continue to be awed by the enormous amount of data he had. Think of it! I was one of nearly 12 million people in the U.S. armed forces at the time—yet he knew my name; my place of birth; was off only a couple of days on date of birth; my parents' names, my wife's name and date and place of birth; was off only a day or so on when I entered the

Appendix 1

service (and where I was first assigned); what bases I had been assigned to; when the crew and I arrived in the United Kingdom and when we were assigned to our base; when and where our final mission took off and its target; and a lot more. There were some gaps in his data, of course—which was why he spent so much time interrogating me. Things like recognition signals, aiming points on the ground, and such—things which only the navigator or the pilot would have reason to know.

Of course, as a longtime newsman, I was clear as to how a good part of this stuff was gathered: You remember those signs you used to see, about "the enemy is listening?" I had communicated with my wife, my folks, some business acquaintances, as I moved to various places. I suppose these folks talked to others about this—and somebody was picking up the scraps.

I'm also sure they really didn't have that much information on everybody—though they tried very hard to imply that they did. Obviously, the most likely candidates for "prisonership" would be people in the air arm—hence they probably concentrated on these folks (myself included).

The enormity of the task of collecting such information, picking up all the scraps and pieces and putting them together, to say nothing of the purely military stuff, still awes me. And still makes me consider that the vaunted German thoroughness does really exist.

That's something for military planners to think about, in the future.

◆ ◆ ◆

I should also mention our "intelligence" efforts. In this, I believe we were able to be useful to our own forces, too.

First of all, as each new "cadre" of prisoners came in, we examined them very carefully—albeit as informally and in the least-threatening or official way we could.

Mostly this was done by senior officers among us—though some others (myself, for instance) also took part.

We had two reasons:

1. The Germans were forever trying to sneak in undercover people this way—after all, it was possible, it seemed to them, since we were all prisoners and all of the men wore uniforms, or pieces of uniforms, of our armies. Many of these people were actually German soldiers or intelligence officers, but many had lived in the U.S., and most could correctly answer simple queries such as "who is Babe Ruth?", or "how are the Dodgers doing?", or something. Many were also familiar, to some extent, with a lot of U.S. localities as well. And they claimed to be from some outfit or another, perfectly legitimately and we couldn't check; all were loaded with information as to how and where they were captured.

The German intelligence theory—and it was quite correct—was that I wouldn't tell any official questioner anything about our "G" boxes or such things. But in a camp-compound argument, among a bunch of prisoners, I might volunteer some information that might be useful, in the belief that those

Appendix 1

with me were also captured prisoners. It was hard to spot these people (an accent, in itself, wasn't remarkable, given the diversity of most Americans), but we always could find some among our group who came from the claimed town or area, had been in the claimed outfit, or something, so we could check a good deal into these stories.

When we found one that we thought wasn't quite legitimate, we couldn't just kick him out, beat him up, or otherwise single him out—that would have blown the cover of our whole effort. What we could and did do, however, was simply to see that this fellow got no information—and eventually, the Germans would remove him, since he was of no use to them.

A second reason was that many of these new arrivals, in their wanderings about Germany and occupied countries, had observed things like milk-cows pulling wagons, the condition of the soldiery and their equipment, and such—which could add up to some useful picture of the condition of the German Army and its components; the local economy, and the rest.

More, some of them could confirm some of our own information as to the conditions of battle and the like—to add to what we could guess as to the progress of the war.

2. When we had gathered what we could, supplemented by some information of our own (such as that brought back by the Russians), we put it together. Then we used the Swiss or other couriers to carry it out—never involving them directly, but slipping material into their briefcases or packages whenever we could.

I've never been sure whether any—or how much—of this ever got back to our own lines, but we felt we were doing something, anyway.

Appendix 2

♦

Our Escape Committees, and Work on Escapes

I didn't include anything—for obvious reasons—in my diary about our "Escape Committee", or the many and various escape plans that were constantly being advanced, worked on, or abandoned.

The fact that such a group existed was known to all of us—but never mentioned, anywhere, even by reference. It was well established, however, that if anyone had any idea of escaping, or any plan, he must first contact the committee, and get approval as well as any assistance available, if the idea was approved

The committee itself was a shadowy group, made up of a very few of our brightest and most daring—all of them carefully approved by Colonel Spivey and our own top brass. If the plan was not approved—because it was too harebrained, or too daring, or presumed too much out of ignorance or whatever—that was supposed to be the end of it, and was, at least in most cases. The rationale was clear: Any escape of more than one or two of us would certainly trigger intensified searches and probably punishments for the rest of us. Thus, such an escape would have to be covered as well as possible in order to give the escapees as much time as possible to get away before a search started; consequences would almost certainly be visited on the rest of us, thus the effort had to have some chance of success to make it worth that consequence.

Such "consequences", we learned, could be extremely severe—as the war wore on, and as evidence increasingly indicated that our captors were not to be on the winning side, they had become more and more nervous, and wouldn't hesitate to summarily execute almost anyone who might have had any connection with the escape. We had a good example of that: Just a few days before the crew and I arrived at Sagan, there had been what was later known as "the great escape"—some 76 men got away, many of them Americans. Every single one of them—with one exception, so far as I know—was recaptured within a day or so. All of them were present with us, within a day.

One morning, during the routine "Appel", German guards went through the ranks, picked out all of the ex-escapees, and then proceeded to shoot in the head every third one of them, right before us.

Appendix 2

Up to then, it had been a sort of game. You escaped, were caught, thrown into solitary confinement for a couple of days, and everybody had a good laugh. Now, it wasn't a game anymore. The escapes stopped dead and for a while after that, I can assure you.

Nevertheless, the "committee" kept on working.

It had a couple of jobs that were ongoing:

First importance, perhaps, was an attempt to prepare some sort of food that wouldn't spoil and could be carried easily. It was believed that the farther an escapee could get from the camps before he had to take a chance of contacting German civilians for food (or the chance of being caught while trying to steal it) the better—and least likely to be turned in. And, since we had no means of refrigeration or any other means of preserving anything (and not much chance to carry much), the committee worked hard to develop a sort of "jerky"—stringy stuff, made out of whatever we had, smoked or dried or something, that could be chewed on and provide some sort of nourishment.

A second point was maps—those we had, with meticulous copies as best we could, so that an escapee could find his way without having to make inquiries. That would include roads and byways, locations of cities and towns, some idea of where railways ran, river transportation, and whatever else we could gather.

Third was physical condition. None of us—after months of the diet we had in the camps, was what you might call robust. But the escapee had to have enough physical strength to walk for miles, hide out in terrible weather, keep going, without breaking down and needing medical attention. So, potential escapees were required to keep up a course in physical exercise for some time before an escape.

Finally, there was the need to supply as much information as we could get about troop concentrations to be avoided, locations of supply depots and such. Some of this information we could get from other prisoners, the Russians, for instance, whom the Germans used as labor troops, got out of the camp for a bit almost daily; some of it from our own people who managed to observe things as they were brought into the camp, some even from the Swiss Red Cross people who visited the camp from time to time.

And, of course, the means of escape. Those triple rows of electrified barbed wire and gun-studded guard towers were a formidable barrier, as well as the "deadline"—and of course we couldn't simply start digging holes in plain sight. So the solution was tunneling—usually from some point within the compound but as close to the wire as we could get.

One thing in our favor was the fact that the whole area was underlain—for many feet down—with nothing but sand. We found that this sand, if it stayed damp, would hold shape rather well, didn't require much in the way of shoring or support, so long as the tunnel itself was reasonably oval, and not too large.

There were the twin problems of hiding the entrances, and disposing of the excavated material. Hiding the entrances was fairly easy; we took up floor

Appendix 2

boards in the barracks, replaced them each day, so that—unless a guard noticed a hollower sound in one section—the hole was effectively covered. (They found most of them, eventually.)

Disposal was another problem: You couldn't just dump a lot of fresh sand anywhere—it would be noticed and investigated at once. The British weren't as clever as we in this: Their solution was to sew up the ends of pants and underwear, fill them with sand, and store them in the spaces between the roof and the ceiling of their barracks—where, eventually, the weight would collapse the whole thing.

We did it better: Each man, after digging a while, would fill his pockets and any other such receptacle with sand, then, as he walked around the compound, just push it out, a little at a time, as he walked. I'll bet we raised the level of that compound a foot or more in the time I was there, just doing this. But it wasn't so easily noticed—and to have a few grains of sand in your clothes wasn't unusual anyway, in that camp.

Another problem was level: It seemed that no matter how careful we were, eventually the tunnel we were digging would slant upward, and we'd suddenly come out of the ground at the wrong place. That is, until some further genius among us invented a level—no more than a water filled pan—that would keep us on a level course as we went.

The most elaborate escape tunnel I worked on, late in the game, was one that started from a shaft we sank right in the middle of the family-sized "abort" that served us all, a sort of 40-holer. We figured that no one would look for a tunnel starting there. And we were right. More, there was nothing remarkable about a lot of men going in and out of the Abort, staying awhile, or whatever. We all had dysentery.

I won't attempt to describe the messy, smelly job we had sinking that shaft, but after we did it, it was certainly successful. Inside the tunnel, deep enough now to maintain dampness and thus hold its shape, we even rigged electric lights and a rope-activated system to bring excavated material to a central point.

It would have been successful, too, except that one day, after we had gotten the tunnel almost to the outer wire fence, some German soldier, operating a horse-drawn dray in the "no man's land" area (where he shouldn't have been), fell into it, and thus the whole thing was discovered.

Appendix 3

♦

Our Radio Receiver
How It Was Built, How Concealed from German Searches

I've mentioned several times and at several places that we had a radio receiver, but never dared to give any description or anything else.

Perhaps it would be well, now, to explain a little more:

That radio was a crystal set, put together before we arrived at the camp. It needed no elaborate tubes, wires or anything.

What we did to conceal it was simple enough—and it never seemed to have occurred to our captors:

Each man in two very select groups carried a piece of the dismantled set—I, for example, might have a couple of screws in my pockets, another fellow a short bit of wire, somebody else a little piece of tinfoil, etc.

We would meet, as casually as we could, some place, each day when the British Broadcasting Company (BBC) scheduled its daily broadcasts of communiques from Allied Supreme Headquarters, assemble the set, and copy down or try to remember what was said. Then, we dismantled the set completely—each man again taking away some small piece—until the next time.

Thus, if the Germans had searched any of us, they would find only meaningless bits of stuff—certainly not enough to indicate the presence of a radio.

Why they never thought of this, I don't know—maybe they guessed, and figured they could never find enough to nail anybody or anything.

So far as I know, they were always looking for a complete radio of some kind—thus they never found it.

Of course they knew we had such a thing, and it frightened them.

Not understanding us or our military very well, what they were afraid of was that we might receive orders from our own headquarters, might be ordered to create an uprising or other trouble that could tie down some of their troops at some critical point.

We were a couple of thousand men, and certainly could have caused trouble. But we would also, and certainly, have been massacred quickly—we had nothing in the way of weapons (other than home-made clubs and knives), no match

Appendix 3

for the 50-caliber machine guns and other armaments in the six guard towers or available to the guard forces. Hence any diversion we could have made would have been both very brief and very bloody. I am certain that our headquarters would never have ordered such a thing anyway—there is even some doubt in my mind that we would have responded, given the enormous odds against us.

But the Germans were quite mindful of the fact that their own troops might very well have responded, even though blindly and with no hope, to such an order.

So it frightened them.

As to the information we got: The Germans did broadcast to us, via loudspeakers, the daily communique by their own OKW (Oberkommando der Wehrmacht). We were well aware that both the OKW and the BBC broadcasts were full of propaganda and efforts to put things in the best possible light, but by comparing the two, we could arrive at a reasonably close approximation of the real truth of what was actually happening.

That comparison, then, was the basis of the "good news today" comments which were all I dared to note in the diary itself, at the time. They meant, of course, that the Allies had won some ground, or a victory, or had advanced closer to us.

Two things should be considered in this whole matter of information:

1. The propaganda aspect.

As a former news reporter and editor, I was fascinated by the technique employed by the German government. They didn't lie. What they did was not give the full information. For example, they'd announce plainly that "there is fighting today at someplace or other," without giving any further details as to how the fighting was going. And most importantly, without giving any indication of the locations where the fighting was going on.

I suppose to the average German—without maps, and certainly given the obscurity of the location mentioned—the announcement had little significance: No more, in fact, than if the U.S. Command announced that "there is fighting today at Peapack, N.J."—unless you knew the area well, that wouldn't mean very much. But if you had a map, thus could see that Peapack is only 20 miles from New York City (or for that matter, if fighting was going on at Poolesville, Md., which is only 30 miles from Washington, D.C.) the fact of the fighting then would have significance to a casual reader as to the real importance that the "enemy" had gotten that far.

2. The only real "propaganda" that I saw was an effort to paint allied forces as barbarians of some kind, in order to frighten German citizens. For example, some of the few German newspapers we managed to obtain carried almost daily front-page cartoons, showing big-toothed, nose-ringed, vicious Negro pilots, in attack planes, joyfully attacking German civilians. As we well knew, most of the black pilots were even better trained than we were; were a sort of elite among the blacks, and certainly not any more savage than any of us.

Appendix 3

Another aspect of our intelligence gathering was maps. The Germans didn't supply us with any such things—but somehow, our people had managed to put together a fair collection of such maps, which we kept carefully concealed, on which we would trace what was going on.

Some of these maps had been smuggled in: All of us in air crew were provided with "escape packets" when we took off—small packages containing some candy, some cigarettes, and fairly well detailed maps, usually printed on silk so that they could appear to be handkerchiefs or scarves. In most cases, German interrogators were looking out for such things and confiscated them (they did that in the case of myself and our crew). But a few escaped such efforts, and found their way to us, where they were used as basis for some of the remarkably detailed charts and maps our "escape committee" managed to put together both for our own uses and to be supplied to anyone who tried to escape from the camps, to guide such people to points where they could expect help.

Appendix 4

♦

Tin Can Carpentry
How It Was Done, Improvised Tools, etc.

At several points, I have mentioned the fact that we made many plates, pans and other utensils out of the tin cans that brought in the food that the Red Cross sent us.

The method was simple enough—though, again, a testament to ingenuity. What we did was this:

We discovered that if we took the empty cans, and cut off the "bead" where the side meets the top, we could then produce a roll of quite presentable metal. Using kitchen knives, handles and whatever we could find, we could then hammer these rolls into flat plates of metal—perhaps three inches wide by close to a foot long.

Then, by placing the edges of our plates on the edge of a table or any other reasonably square edge, and using a knife-handle as a hammer, we could create a standing edge perhaps an eighth of an inch deep, along the full edges of each metal sheet. Putting any two of these together, so that the upstanding edge of one was inside the downstanding edge of the next, we could then hammer down the two edges, thus forming a creditable joint much as the old-fashioned "flat seams" or "standing seams" were made on old "tin" roofs of houses. Doing this, thus, we could create a single sheet of metal to almost any size—crimping up the corners for a couple of inches, if desired, thus to create a pan or plate. Of course, these contraptions leaked a bit, but cooking in them a couple of times and not being too careful about washing (which we couldn't do, anyway, because of lack of hot water), would provide enough sediment to seal the joints fairly well—thus we had pans, pots and plates that could be used.

Eventually, of course, we went beyond plates and pans. One "Kriegie" manufactured a washing machine out of the cans, with paddles and driven by a small windmill also fashioned of this "tin", another even made a clock, with gears and weights also made of the "tin". About this time, however, the Germans began depriving us of the cans—I think in the fear that we would some-

Appendix 4

how manufacture a tank or a real weapon—and we might very well have done so, I believe.

In any event, the stuff we made—which, by the way included stoves and similar devices—served us well. And it is a skill that I have used since, in cobbling up things around the house.

Appendix 5

♦

Games for Amusement
Confusing the Guards for Laughs

There was a game we played for quite a while—which the Germans never understood, I know. They couldn't imagine that we did it for no reason except for fun, and to make the days seem a bit less boring.

What you did was to corner one of the "ferrets" or one of the other German personnel who were constantly wandering around inside the compound.

When you had the man cornered, you began very serious conversation in German—replete with gestures, finger pointing and all the rest. Except, of course, what you were saying—with as much emphasis and solemnity as possible—was absolute nonsense. Most of us had learned a little German—enough to inquire where the nearest toilet was, or whether the water was drinkable—so, you just strung together all of these words, in no order, and with no sense at all. But you did it, as I said, with the utmost apparent sincerity, raising your voice at appropriate points to indicate a question, roaring out other things as positive statements.

The man would stand absolutely still for a time, wrinkling his brows as he tried to figure out what in creation you were saying, or what you wanted.

You couldn't keep it up for long—the man would catch on, or you couldn't keep a straight face. So, after a minute or so, you threw up your hands in apparent despair, muttered something like "Dummkopf!", and walked off, shaking your head at the obvious stupidity of a person who couldn't understand his own language!

As I said, I don't believe the Germans ever understood that we did this just for amusement—nothing else.

And they never figured out what to do about it either.

There were a couple of other things we did, too—also for nothing more than amusement and diversion.

As I noted, most of the German soldiery we came into contact with could speak or understand English—though all would deny it. But one or two actually and demonstrably really could not.

Appendix 5

One of these was a large, pink-faced, curly-haired blond fellow—one of a type who had been on the south end of a northbound plow, probably, when the Wehrmacht came along and grabbed him. I don't believe he had any idea of what the war was about, or who the Nazis were—or where America was, in fact. But he tried to be pleasant.

Someone taught him to say:

"Good morning! I am a fool!" as a proper greeting.

He did this, happily, every morning for a week or two—basking in the smiles he elicited with his greeting, never realizing what he was saying.

At least he did until some of the other Germans realized what he was doing.

The man disappeared totally at that point. We never saw him again.

Suppose he was taken out and shot, or sent to the Russian front, or something, for disgracing the Fatherland. Never found out.

Under the heading of (sort of) "fun" should be another thing we did.

I need to explain: Every couple of weeks, the Germans brought into the camp a sort of "honey wagon"—a truck which mounted a large metal tank, a hose and a pump—which was brought to the 40-holer "aborts" to pump out the material that had accumulated in the concrete tanks below the seats. (By the way, this material was then taken directly to nearby fields and pumped onto the ground as a form of fertilizer, without any treatment. This was a reason—once we learned of it—for us to try to scrub or peel anything in the way of food [such as potatoes] that we were issued by our captors.

Anyway, this "honey wagon" was always driven by a German private, with another private as a helper, and supervised by a very important German sergeant, who rode along.

We made a practice, whenever this rig appeared, to announce its presence with shouts of "Hier kommt der Scheissenpanzer fuehrer"—a phrase that really doesn't need any explanation or translation.

The title and accompaniment of the shouting always visibly annoyed the sergeant, who considered himself to be an important functionary. And it always got us a series of glares, bristling mustachio, and hard-eyed looks, accompanied by German curses.

But we did it anyway—just for fun.

Appendix 6

♦

Character Studies of German Soldiery
How Organized, How Obeyed

A couple of instances of the caliber of the German soldiery and the discipline under which they operated:

At Sagan, the daily "Appels" (roll calls) were conducted by us prisoners lining up, in a reasonable approximation of military formations, usually in rows of 10 men from front to back.

Once we were lined up, under command of our own officers, a German soldier—usually a corporal—would march along the front, counting not individual persons, but rows of men, then multiply his total by 10, thus arriving at a "count". (This practice, by the way, made it fairly easy to cover an escape for a while, when needed—men from other rows could filter into any row that was short, once the guard had passed, so that he always saw full rows of 10 as he marched along.)

Anyway, on one dank, cold morning, we went through this procedure (all the rows were full, incidentally, except for a few who were sick; there had been no recent escapes). At the end, the corporal came up with a total that didn't agree with the roster held by his sergeant, who witnessed the procedure.

After bawling out the corporal, the sergeant went through the same exercises to make his own count. And, when he was through, his count didn't agree with that of the corporal—or with the roster.

At this point appeared a lieutenant, who figured out what was happening after a lot of gesticulation and discussion. He proceeded to bawl out the corporal and the sergeant—and then he himself marched through the count.

When he was through, it appeared that his count not only didn't agree with those of his underlings, but also didn't agree with the roster's figures.

There followed an extensive period of shouting, swearing and gesticulation, until a German captain appeared. He proceeded to bawl everybody out, then lined up the lieutenant, the sergeant and the corporal, and smacked each man in the face. Such a gesture, in our army, would have earned the captain a handful of his own teeth, I suppose—but the Germans stood there and took it without a word or gesture.

Appendix 6

Then the captain himself made a count and found that his count not only didn't agree with those of the others, but also didn't jibe with the roster.

The four of them stood around then, for a while, arguing. Finally, the captain announced that his count was correct, everyone else came to attention and saluted, and the whole bunch marched off. We were then dismissed—nobody having in fact come up with the right count.

It would have been funny, but it was cold, damp and dispiriting.

But a good demonstration of how the German military mind worked.

Appendix 7

◆

Some Scenes from Camps
How Senegalese Cursed Out Guards, etc.

Another scene I will long remember. This at Moosburg, only a few days before Patton's Third Army reached us:

I had been somewhere in that depressing camp, and was walking back to the barracks we called home, when I came upon a group of Senegalese troops, under direction of their own sergeant, and under the eye of a machine-pistol-armed German "superman" (a tiny figure, maybe 5'5" tall). The Senegalese were digging some kind of a trench. Though it was now obvious that the war was over and Germany had been defeated, the guard troops had had no other orders, so just went on doing whatever they had been doing, anyway.

The Senegalese—all of them huge men, all of them more than 6 feet tall and almost equally broad across the shoulders, all of them blacker than coal, it seemed to me—were getting orders from the German through their own sergeant, as I noted, a man who wasn't working himself, but stood to one side, observing.

The sergeant (they were French troops, of course) was an enormous man, maybe 6'6" tall, wide shoulders, and also very black, and he spoke nearly perfect French to his men and anyone else. As I came near, I could hear him doing what I still think is probably the very best job of cursing I've ever heard: Not a single dirty word, but he was going back into that German's ancestry about three generations, and then forward another generation or two, calling down upon the family some of the worst penalties that could be imagined. And he was doing it in a soft, gentle voice, punctuated with smiles that showed his startlingly white teeth, bowing occasionally to the guard (who clearly had no idea of what the sergeant was saying, and thus bowed and smiled back).

I was standing a bit to one side, where the German couldn't see me directly. The sergeant obviously realized that I knew what he was saying—so he winked at me a couple of times, in the course of his discourse. And, after a minute or two, I left—largely for fear that I would begin to laugh, and thus give the whole thing away.

A very enlightening encounter—and one that I can still recall as a point of amusement.

Index

♦

A

air raids, 49, 59, 91, 109, 111, 117, 124
airfields
    British, 1
    German, 31, 90, 129
airplanes,
    American, 2-4, 111, 117-118, 122
    German, 31, 89, 91, 92
Alkmaar, Holland, 8-9
Amsterdam, Holland, 9
animals, 6, 14, 49, 68, 98
Appel (roll call), 19-20, 23, 49, 105, App. 6
Applegate, Lt., 58, 68, 85, 104
Armistice Day, 1944, 69
Arnheim, Holland, 53, 90

B

B-17 bombers, 49, 117
B-24 bombers,
    crash, 3-6
    description, 2-3
    flight mission, 3-4
    overhead, 117, 118, 122
barter, 29, 119, 123, 125
Bascom, Lt., 68, 70, 104
Bellaria, Germany, 72, 101
Bingen, Germany, 12
birthday, 33
British prisoners, 17, 19-20
Bunch, Lt. Bill, 70
Burau, Germany, 95

C

Campbell, Maj., 19-20
capture, 6-10
casualties, 7-9, 119
Catlin, Lt. Al, 123
Chemnitz, Germany, 102
Christmas, 1944, 78-82
Coblenz, Germany, 12
Cole, Lt. Gordon, 129
Cole, "King", Sq. Ldr. RAF, 17, 20
Cole, Lt. Robert E., xiv, 1-4, 9-10, 14-17, 20, 50, 129, 133
Cologne, Germany, 12
Currie, S/Sgt. John, xiv, 7, 18

D

Dachau, Germany, 63
Delaney, Lt. Ronald, 46, 50, 73, 77, 86
diseases,
    See Medical conditions and services
Dresden, Germany, 22
Dulag Luft, Germany, 16, 31

E

Easter, 1945, 120
Eatinger, Lt. Cy, 58, 68, 115
Edison, Lt. Charles, 101
education, 25-26, 46, 76-77, 80-81, 84-85
Eindhoven, Holland, 9
escape plans and attempts, 86, App. 2

F

fads, 45, 78, 93
Farthing, Lt. Harold, 117
First, Lt. Dave, 101, 122, 124
Fisher, Lt. Don, 122
food, 9-11, 18, 27, 47, 50, 77, 87, 92, 97, 99, 104, 115
Foodaco, 29
Frankfurt, Germany, 12
French prisoners, 103, 113, 121
Friebus, Germany, 98
FW-190 German airplane, 31, 92

— 150 —

Index

G

Geneva Convention, 17, 28, 50, 90, 110
George, Lt. J. P., 20-21, 23, 108, 113, 115
German prisoners, 29
Gettino, Lt. Nick, 55
Gomez, Lt., 54, 99
Good, Col., 124, 127
Goza, Lt. Curt, 122
Greenquist, Lt. Bob, 101, 123
guards, German, 6-13, 23, 26, 35, 98, App. 5-7
Gwinner, Lt. Fred, 100

H

Hackett, Maj., 17
Halbau, Germany, 94-95, 98
Halesworth, England, 1
Hamilton, Lt., 91
Hart, Sgt. Frank A., xiv, 1-4, 93, 133
Hoorn, Holland, 7

I

Independence Day, 1944, 14
inspection, 34
interrogation, 14-16, App. 1

J

Jensen, Lt. Bob, 124

K

Kelly, Lt. Pat, 60, 79, 96
Kennedy, Col., 101
Kethley, Lt. Jerry, 89, 93
Kramer, Lt., 58

L

Labor Day, 1944, 46
Leipzig, Germany, 22
Leonard, Sgt. W. K. (Jim), xiv, 1-4, 9, 18
library, 25, 48
living conditions, 25-27, 33-35, 79, 103, 104-108, 110, 121

M

Maastricht, Holland, 9
Manching, Germany, 129
Martin, Col., 93
medical conditions and services, 57, 80, 83, 86, 104, 120

Meninger, Germany, 61
money, 28-29, 78
Moore, Lt. Bob, 102
Moos, Sgt. Jim J., xiv, 1-4, 8, 11, 18, 133
Moosburg, Germany, 99-129
Mulligan, Lt. Tom, 46, 73
Munich, Germany, 102, 125
musical activities, 26, 34, 52
Muzkau, Germany, 95-99

N

New Year's Day, 1945, 84-85
newspapers, 26, 51, 91, 109, 128
Nissen huts, 1, 2
Nuremberg, Germany, 101-103, 121, 123

O

Obermasfeld, Germany, 61
Oberursel, Germany, 13-17
overcrowding, 31, 34-35, 57, 59, 105, 110, 121

P

P51, 111, 117
parachuting, 4-5
Patterson, Lt. Tony, Anzac, 128
Patton, Gen. George, 118, 128
Perkinson, Lt. Bill, 121
Post, Lt. Robert B., xiv, 1-4, 7-8, 14, 18, 20, 54, 69, 129, 133
Powrie, Derrick, Anzac, 128
prisoner ingenuity, 24, 26-27, 52, 113
prisoner movement,
    See purges (incoming prisoners)
    See transportation of prisoners
propaganda, 31, 51, 73
protecting power, 106, 109
Purinton, Lt. Col., 30
purges (incoming prisoners), 31-32, 46, 55, 63, 66

R

radio, 52, 89, 125, App. 3
recreation,
    card games, 32, 57, 83
    chess, 54
    drama, 29, 32, 54, 63, 76
    movies, 29, 34, 71
    sports, 28, 30, 46, 80, 83, 89, 92
Red Cross, 18-19, 21, 26, 64, 80
religious services, 26, 60, 81, 106, 120, 123
rescue, 126
Russian prisoners, 21, 71

Index

S

Sagan, Germany (Stalag III), 22-93
   description, 23-24
   entry into, 22-23
Santora, S/Sgt. Joe F., xiv, 7-10, 61
Saunders, Flt. Lt., David, RAF, 17
searches and seizures, 6, 18, 49, 125
Shore, Lt. Sid, 73
Siegfried Line, 58, 63
slang, 30
Smart, Lt. David L., xiv, 1-4, 7-10, 123
Smith, Col., 106
Sorenson, S/Sgt. Jack D., xiv, 7, 18
Spivey, Col. D. T., 23, 27, 60, 65, 93
Spremberg, Germany, 100-101
Stuttgart, Germany, 102, 122

T

Thanksgiving Day, 1944, 74-75
tin-can carpentry, 24, 52, 77, 109, 113, App. 4
transportation of prisoners, 6-10, 22, 90, 93-102

U

Utrecht, Holland, 9

V

Valentine's Day, 1945, 106-108
Vanaman, Brig. Gen. A. W., 28
Venlo, Holland, 10-12

W

War news,
   about Austria, 76, 86, 123
   about Balkans, 35, 47, 60
   about Belgium, 46, 47, 63
   about France, 31, 35, 47, 86
   about Germany, 57, 58, 61, 69, 72, 81, 109, 111, 115, 118, 123-124
   about Goebbels, 66, 86
   about Himmler, 61, 123
   about Hitler, 86
   about Holland, 47, 53, 72
   about Hungary, 57, 58, 62, 76, 82
   about Italy, 76
   about Luxembourg, 79
   about Poland, 88-89, 91
   about Roosevelt, 69, 109, 122
Webb, Lt., 91, 113

Wetzlar, Germany, 19-21
Willetts, Cmdr., RAF, 124, 127
work, 34, 64, 73

Y

Yalta, Allied conference, 109
YMCA, 25, 64, 80

Z

Zwichau, Germany, 102-103